THE NAIF

Valerie Hsiung

UDP :: Dossier

PRAISE FOR *THE NAIF*

Halfway between Kafka's Singer and Melville's Scrivener, Hsiung's *Naif* wields syntax as both tuning fork and sensor, sounding a singular diphthong at once cosmic and quasi-comic. With minute adjustments to eyeline and plumbline, this naif induces us to perceive human interaction as at once present and potential, threat and promise, banquet and gambit, culture and cult.

—Joyelle McSweeney

A philosophical rumination that pulls us all the way into its depths, *The Naif* is an abstract painting made of words and sentences and punctuation or lack thereof, a distant memory whose skin you get to touch and feel as you attempt to find your way through its centers and peripheries. *The Naif* is an attempt for "reconciliation" between what we try to do in life while we have "already gone off course," while we navigate an intimate piece of clothing dangling on a chair, cheese, mouse, juice gone bad, a lamp, a gift

shop, all the what and the who of the everyday guiding us toward the word "transcend." Kneading a slippery "new way of life" into a shape that is shifting and grounding, Valerie Hsiung shares with us her being in and out of community, in intimacy and in selfness. She invites us to "conduct ourselves according to the pulse of each other without losing the pulse of ourselves" while we immerse ourselves in the pulse of her beautiful language offering.
—*Poupeh Missaghi*

Is it innocence to think that if you hold onto something long enough (community, relationship, attention) the habitual will give way to the extraordinary? The "person of insouciance" relating this logbook narrative evolves through the willful and unsuspecting ironies that threaten to foil the aim of artists and revolutionaries alike. *The Naif* so deranges intention with particulars—that is, with wonder—as to turn everyday fact into speculative fiction. A new way of living may yet prevail, thanks to Hsiung's encouragement, akin to the spores of a mushroom, or to winning the lottery, waiting for us all along, as though in advance of the beginning.

—*Roberto Tejada*

Day 24 / 10 at night

We are planning something extraordinary. That's the reason for the animals, the constellations, the moss, the fairy tales, going into a cyber main street, prioritizing how and what we were sourcing. I had to do a fair amount of research. A lot of the skills I took to prepare for the planning of this event were not wholly unrelated to the skills I acquired in my years of training.

The irony is that we never planned to plan something extraordinary. In fact, that was the whole point. That what was extraordinary was what we had not been planning but doing all along. What ended up mixing this notion up was the fact that it wasn't solely our affair to plan or to not plan. Even though we agreed from the get go we would have our own boundaries and stick to them, we would have our own bottom lines, each step along the way a new idea would enter into the planning process and it would become more "extraordinary." In the beginning, often the new idea wasn't our own idea by any measure and so it was difficult to know how to put ourselves in it and so it felt far from extraordinary. Generally, it just felt like we were taking it because that's what you did. Again, all of this is contrary to our original boundaries, what we initially agreed upon.

This is what stressed me out at first. Suddenly all of our original plans to not plan something extraordinary were thrown out of the window and we were just being swept away by this and that and I could already sense the resentment brewing. And then the more I thought about it the more I noticed that I wanted to think more about all the little details and at first I wasn't sure if it was because it was eroding away my boundaries and that was a bad thing or if it was readjusting my boundaries and that was ok because maybe our original boundaries weren't so well thought out after all, maybe we were just sticking to it because we got the idea that's what was best, that's who we were, and that's what we wanted. Like, are we frivolous people? Certainly sometimes, and maybe we should be glad to be so. What was at first one person's idea of extraordinary and thus our idea of a poverty of life and dreaming became less a matter of opposites and more a matter of deciding what was for us, what percentage of our total caring would go into this particular portion, what of this extraordinary would arrive from our own doing, our own meticulous dreamed doing.

I have never planned something on this level. The more I go deeper into the planning, the more this extraordinary event begins to dwarf me. I think I return here in part because there is something to be said about this dwarfing. Or rather there is something I have sensed before elsewhere related to this aspect of being dwarfed by something both extraordinary and entirely received, something entered into without any intention, entered into as though being swept into it by something ordinary, and it is actually this combination of effects that results in something pathetically extraordinary. It is the fact that time is lost as one is dwarfed that something extraordinary arises but that's not all it is either. It's really this frivolous poverty as time is lost as one is being dwarfed and it's really the movement from a person that is insouciant and capable of letting other people down and especially those who really don't deserve it and it's really the movement from this person of insouciance and immaturity amidst a frivolous poverty amidst time lost amidst carnage changing into a mindset that is extraordinary. Actually, we see the person become a mindset become a person and that is extraordinary.

Day 29 / 11 in the morning

I have come to the realization that it might not be totally crazy to expect an uneven contribution between the community members. Especially in the event that we are bound by the old neighborhood, where prices may have lowered recently but are still exponentially greater than the next twenty richest neighborhoods combined. If we love trees and fresh air so much, why don't we go somewhere that s not even compiled in the twenty richest neighborhoods, not even in the top one thousand. I only get one vote. I voted for us to leave, go somewhere very far. I would be most happy in the desert where wildness isn't even measured by a density of greenery, where greenery is different and I am in love with a different landscape. Nope. I only get one vote and we have talked about this many times until it escalated into a fight. It always boils down to, I don't have any family, I do, so what, I want to stay near my family, you lied to me, you made it seem like we would live our own life. (/) The people who want to be so tough feel like play-dough to me sometimes.

Lately (…/,) I've been thinking how I had this bird in my hand and it was a strong bird but it was a strong bird in my hands, happened to be sick and I can't remember if I handled it correctly. Lately when we have been lying, lying in bed I think I can't believe how close I came to handling it all incorrectly. It's one of those questions, like, let's say we just continued to be swept away effectively, stayed where we've always been, stayed close to one side, reproduced, reproduced while I attend this women's reading group, radical reproduction, what could we not do that we could do otherwise? I have to pause(.) B/but then quickly(.) I remember many things.

Lately, when we've been lying in bed together I say, this time, we'll make a baby! We can get the sperm. We can get the sperm and then we make a baby. So funny, without a penny to my name, and here I am thinking of reproduction. Without a penny to my name and trying to live in a way that doesn't take and take, and here I am thinking of baby, so frivolously. But then(.) I remember how much we die(,/.) how easy it is to die(.) A/and it makes me feel less guilty.

Day 64 / noon

What is the purpose of all the bells and whistles, of all the ceremonial aspects of this game. Why isn't our love enough? So many things have had to sync up for it to all work out. That's why it's hazy and they call things miracles. That's why this would have to be a miracle. The entire production. So many timelines have to be in sync for the miracle to occur, you wonder if the miracle is a miracle at all, since it would seem a lot of foresight and planning are at work in making the timelines match up at all.

You could say in a way that the entire question of the community rests in part on the ability to make sure not a single item is out of sync between timelines. Even when the entire reason for preparing so fully for the community right now, the entire work of what the community is, that's the work of preparing for a possible community, is really wrapped up in potentially fucking up the entire timeline, or the syncing up of timelines. Even when the syncing up of timelines still might not prove to be any miracle in and of itself, for what is the point of syncing up the timelines at all when the community is gone, or when the community has turned its back on you, or worse, you have turned your back on the community. Maybe less dramatic but perhaps more dire is the risk that the syncing up of timelines will have been for naught, miracle or no miracle, if everyday is an uphill struggle. But wait, isn't that what you turn to the community for? Isn't that what constitutes the community? This uphill motion?

It's like we know where there is abundance of actual life there is also a tremendous uncertainty of maybe surviving, and where there is an abundance of luxury, there is actually a tremendous dearth of actual life. We say we recognize when others speak in extremes, when we ourselves speak in a way that sees everything around us so black and white, and then we say these things. Because we see them, clearly. Of course it is something that needs to be pointed out but something that needs to be pointed out does not mean it is true one hundred percent of the time and only that way either.

We've talked about where we want to set up shop. As though the location will ultimately confine us to a static place for a fixed amount of time. As though the location will be crucial in framing what scopes us out or something. In reality, we will be limited by whatever decision we make. We can either prolong the limiting of the decision or we can dive right in and begin limiting it sooner rather than later. Another way to look at it is we can either prolong the choice of making a decision that will undoubtedly have permanent repercussions on the possibility for our miracle timelines to not be a daily uphill battle in some ways or we can set up shop elsewhere and be limited in another way, be limited in prospects alternatively. There is of course no perfect solution and at this point it becomes clear that we will have to come to a mutual agreement, or compromise, on what is the acceptable risk to take. It almost seems that the most acceptable risk to take creates the most amount of daily stress for us. How can that be? How have we done this to ourselves?

It is true there is the opportunity for making something special out of this problem. Yet I have found often that a complete mistake can also easily be perceived, and not wrongly so in fact, as something special. A complete mistake can be very special in a thousand ways. Of course it is true that there are a thousand different forms that this community could take and that if you say no to even two of them, another thing could present itself to you as a form of partaking in the community. At the least it could be something that you tell yourself quite convincingly. And yet it is also true that this specific complete mistake could be just a more glorified version of the very real type of partaking in community which instigated this entire investigation to begin with. What I mean by this is that perhaps in the beginning the type of possible mistake was more poetic in a sense, in that it wasn't so glorified, it was very much a more quiet mistake, and it wouldn't rely so much on merely telling yourself that this was partaking in the community, it wouldn't rely so much on convincing yourself that what you were doing was partaking in the community, because it was. So maybe glorified is the wrong way to put it. Really, the quieter way is likely the more glorified way. And maybe the big mistake, the less poetic mistake, is an opportunity waiting for us.

And maybe since what I'm hearing is that almost it's that the big mistake isn't what you want at all, either out of fear of some unsustainable consequences, out of fear in partaking in the wrong community, maybe because of this you will find a way into other unexpected communities, whether right or wrong, they will be communities nonetheless, and you will have found yourself there out of necessity, and you will have found yourself to be an active participant in order to sustain the unsustainable.

Day 66 / 11 at night

I forget how much we've lost from being born from separate worlds. I have to remind myself not to become angry or disappointed, to just be aware of my frustration which is enough. When I say things over and over again, when I have to explain in a dozen different ways, and still I am not completely conveyed, I have to remind myself. When there is a hole between us, and a time zone, a hole, when we go months without speaking to each other and then I get a letter in the mail, I get angry and feel disappointment. But really I haven't sat long enough with my frustration to allow the frustration to be without turning into anger or disappointment. I am allowed to be angry and disappointed, but then what am I filtering out? What piece missing?

Have we always spoken different languages? When did I start speaking another language? When did I start losing my first language? Part of my frustration is my own, only part. Part of my frustration must be someone else. But all of my anger and disappointment is my own. They will never understand what it is I say completely and yet I speak to them, I speak because of them, the way I speak is ingrained with their silences and their speech. I never knew exactly how they resolved things. I imagine now that they simply did because they had no other choice but to do so. Years later I watched around me as other secrets came out from the cracks of our community and I wondered what secrets we kept from each other. It's possible to hide more when you are away from each other but people hide things from each other every day even when they are right beside one another.

In the space we held with each other in our greater community and in the smaller community units, there was a different measure when it came to comfort and appearance. We had different attachments to tradition. I looked around me for example at a piece of wall and I saw that it could be entirely empty or it could be filled in a number of ways. It could be filled with family photos, blown-up postcards from business travels, or it could be filled with ancestral scrolls, embroidery, calligraphy. But there was never an in-between.

There were members of our great community who were veritable artists for hire, there were members of our great community who each played a part and contributed their small role in what it takes for a whole community to look after one another. We would cook communal meals, we would bring food to each other, we would volunteer, we would drive long distances to pick each other up, we would set alarms in the middle of the night so we would be up and ready to do something for each other. We would share stories of when our parents died and we received a phone call telling us our parents died and we would convey how it felt to cry out every single last tear inside of us. We would listen to community members tell other community members of their family members dying and how it felt to be so far away from them and not to be able to see them ever again and we would listen and hearing these stories we understood what we understood and maybe also what we did not understand. We would listen from the back seat of the car and we would watch from the stool in the kitchen and we would peer down from the landing and we would look at an empty wall or an overcrowded wall and some of us grew a sense of longing that they could not ignore inside them, some of us grew a sense of longing inside that they had the luxury as well to not ignore, and some of us grew a sense of longing that became a type of particularity and this type of particularity became a type of viewpoint on a way of life and this type of viewpoint on a way of life became entwined with appearances as well, all full circle.

Now I think of what it is I am afraid of losing of this community as we begin the new community. I am afraid of losing this frustration because this frustration is rooted in this longing and this longing is rooted in this anger and disappointment and this anger and disappointment is rooted in the lack and the lack is rooted in the ordinary difficulties of most humans. I do not know if I can shun the lifestyles of the first world without spoiling it all. I do not know if I can pick and choose which elements of the first world to shun and which elements of the first world we will take with us without first having been completely spoiled.

It is difficult to know exactly where to draw the line between convenience and thoughtlessness. I went to the convenience store. A nun, former hooker. We say we could go either way, we say we could run in an entirely different direction, into the direction of the oldest technology on earth. Is it because deep down we know there is no happy medium? Or is the happy medium the small town that is big enough to have a general store? A main street.

Yesterday I realized a part of me just can't let go of the crass and the crude and the loudness and the aggression of the community I come from, which is really not representative of the larger community I come from, for what smaller community is, what smaller community can be said to be fully representative of any larger community it is or was a part of, I realized a part of me just can't bear to let go of the crass and the crude and the loudness and the aggression and the playfulness of the way we communicated with each other within this community. I said I know what she means. I know what she means. (//...) I know what she means. (//...) The one didn't get me. Later the one said the one did. But I know the one didn't.

Day 73 / 930 in the morning

I said goodnight(.) and then there was a silence(.) and then the one held my hand and then the one let go and then I heard the one say I don't feel good and I

said where physically or... and the one said yeah kind
of and I said where all over and the one said yeah
and I scratched the one's back and the one said it'll
go away and I had just been thinking how the sound
of something like planes could sometimes be heard
above us and I wondered if I could hear them now or
if it was something else and then I thought it's hard
for me to breathe I can breathe but I'm trying and I
can't tell if I just need a sip of water or if I should
just stay where I am and let it pass and then I said
will the light bother you are your eyes completely
covered and the one said yes and I said I'll only be
a minute go to sleep and then I found my way in the
dark to the bathroom where I realized how loud I was
how loud everything I was was even when trying to be
quiet but I couldn't let that stop me so I continued
and it did only take a minute or I was able to do what
needed to be done at the bare minimum within just
a minute though I could have continued I felt I got
what I needed to get out of it or I felt I did what I
needed to do to not forget to not regret and when I
turned off the bathroom light and walked back into
the bedroom and it was completely dark I paused to
let my eyes readjust and when I felt they had read-
justed enough I still had to fumble slowly around in
the dark and in that time between leaving the bath-
room and getting back to bed I was on my way I was
reaching my hands out I was feeling my way through

and I was having this thought and I wanted to stay there but I couldn't.

Maybe because it was the only part of the day where I had no choice but to be in the dark, like it was good for me or something. Like it was the only part of the twenty four hours we are given where I was there in front or behind something that was like a midpoint between endlessness and a mere sliver. I didn't want to lose that feeling but there was something sweet about risking losing that feeling because inevitably you lose that feeling eventually anyway. Like there was something sweet and genuine about feeling it without grasping it and not staying up to stay inside it consciously but rather to recognize it and then to let it slip away.

Maybe sometimes the way we feel about someone is wrapped up in their inability to be a person we could exist in the same world as us, is wrapped up in the very fact that we live in two totally different worlds and there's actually a wall between the two worlds we live in separately and there's actually more than one wall, there's the wall that separates us and it's made out of cardboard and however flimsy it seems we just don't have the tools to penetrate it or we do but something else would get in the way even if we did get through it, even just another layer of cardboard, and so there's this wall, and then there's another wall, but this wall is made of something else, like the scent of something, or the scent of something associated with another dimension, or maybe this wall is also made of cardboard and it's very easy to move, it's so easy to move or get through it's almost a trick, because overtime we move it or get through it, we find we are still in our own world, or we find that they do not acknowledge our existence no matter how close we get to them, no matter how much a part of the air that they breathe we literally become.

For example, I can know her inside and out, I can be her doppelganger, but I can also not know whether she would ask the kind of question like "will I be better?" because maybe we can be doppelgangers and I can follow her around but maybe my reality doesn't apply to her reality the way her reality now applies to mine.

I wonder if our days pass by faster now actually because the world around us seems faster than it does in stories you hear in history books. Or if it's actually slower because we have more time to kick around stones and just be. Sometimes I think this idea of having more time around to kick stones or gravel is an illusion that the people who have made the world go faster just want us to think because really we are aware of kicking around and really a part of us feels guilty or is aware that this is a treat and being aware that something is a treat means we are aware that something is special that having this time to kick stones around is special when really it is entirely ordinary. I don't even think there is any conspiracy so when I say the people who made the world such and such a way want us to think that what I really mean is it's all rigged but it's not rigged by them it was rigged generations and generations ago by people who never saw it coming by people who did one thing to make their lives easier and can you blame them for that no for there are some things I wouldn't really want to be harder or I really wouldn't want to take more time or I really wouldn't want to have to devise my own little trick to circumvent even if I say I would even if I would pay a week's work of salary now to spend a week's worth of time learning how to do the old way. Funny the time we live in today...

There are so many moving parts to this puzzle and every time it looks like we're nearing the end of the tunnel I see that the tunnel becomes a little longer. Every time I think we've set aside enough into our rainy day fund the weather defies the laws of chances and we get a week extra of rain and then we realize we have nothing left and we have to borrow some more. There are so many moving parts to this puzzle and every time I think I'm not too shabby at handling all the pieces to the puzzle, making sure I keep track of which pieces look like each other, which pieces belong near the border and which pieces belong in another corner, making sure I don't lose a piece to somewhere, I realize I've never done this puzzle before and I realize the puzzle didn't come with a set number of pieces. No, it's the kind of puzzle that you could keep growing if you wanted to, and it's the kind of puzzle that could be done anytime you want it to be done and it's the type of puzzle that you set out somewhere like in a public park and people walk by and people are set up next to you with their own puzzles and you have other people's puzzles to compare it to and you wonder if what you thought was done was really done.

Then one day you're at the park and no one else is there and it's exactly then when you're perfectly content when you realize you really are done with your puzzle that you see the way you've done your puzzle is wrong, it looks complete but it won't hold, there's no way you can actually take it with you anywhere, if that makes sense, there's no way to actually keep it together, show anyone what you've done, all the work you've put into it, all the time, really it was almost for nothing... Maybe at a certain point we'll have figured it out, enough, at least for us to keep it together, at least to a point where enough of it is kept together that it won't matter what we leave behind, it won't matter what gets dropped to the wayside, because enough of the most important will be taken care of. Anyway we draw a line...

Day 30 / 230 in the afternoon

This new way of living has been changing me. I feel it in my inability to think in another way. It's not that I am unable to think differently but I have to try a lot harder. After having shook myself out of an extended dream state, it's hard to just will myself to dream again. What I am calling an extended dream state is one where wherever I am, I can let go, without stopping myself too much. It's hard to differentiate because right now, technically, I am also not stopping myself, but I'm also continually stopping myself in a way. I wonder if I can commit to this new way of living and also take on a single other project. But perhaps project needs to be defined. Until this point, project stood for something other than what it might stand for now. When I say project now, I mean a way of approaching the various assets associated with the old way of life. I do not mean how I eat, how I cook, how I find the clothes to wear, how we get from place to place. These are essential things we need to live and thus I will not fuss over a designation here of project or not project. For example, this morning I added something to our basket. That was fine and not contradictory to our way of life. Baby steps. This morning I also purchased some linens and t-shirts since the only ones we have are very old and have begun to smell no matter how much I clean them. I didn't realize until afterwards how long I had been waiting to do that. What is it about this new way of life that says responsibility is different from Thoreau's conception of it, what is it about this new way of life that says responsibility is not what we think of as responsibility, personal responsibility.

I don't have questions on, are you a good person, self? No, I don't question much on that. And I don't much question either on how do you feel, self, either. It's much less straight-forward than that even though I'm here and there enough to know that there could be something amiss right now, too. It's much less straight-forward about the very straight-forward then. I am starting to question how I ever went so far with the other way of living and how much time I still have to get good at this new one. I sit at the front of the store for example, I sit in front of the little box, no one comes inside the store, there may as well be a sign, a sign like closed all day long, except I know there isn't a sign like that and if there were it wouldn't even say closed. People pass by, of course, they look in... Then they walk on again. At most people stop for a moment longer and they look at themselves in the window like a mirror, like a drink, because these store windows do have an effect of depth, and meantime I just remain here on stool. If I need something from the back of the store, I punch around on the register, count all the bills in it, then I lock it up, look outside to make sure no one nearby could be ever arriving, then I go to the back to get whatever it is I needed to get. That simple. Sometimes, even when I've felt hungry for an hour already, I'll still just stay sitting there, on my still stool, like waiting to be picked up, not waiting for a townsperson to show up, mind you, waiting to be picked up. There is a dance in this aimless indecision, in this almost pointless obstinance that eventually gives in anyway. Then, eventually, even when you're doing nothing you will need the sustenance so I do go to the back and I do make myself a sandwich. Sauerkraut, pickles, mustard, thousand year egg...

Why don't I yell at myself or talk down to myself when I open up the register just to count the bills, why don't I empty the register and buy whatever I can from the store instead of sneaking away little items from the storage closet. If I was upfront about it and honest, I wouldn't have to sneak around. But it's hard to be upfront about things when aimlessness feels so harmless and natural. Besides, eventually we'll have a line all the way around the corner and we won't be able to keep up with demand and I won't have to sneak to the back at all, I'll just be able to take whatever because we're doing so well. And because the store's doing well, that'll mean I'm doing well too. I wonder...

Today we got at least two or three deliveries, I've lost count. So that's the only person I see these days, mail woman. The other day I was watching a singing show on tv, the other day a singing talent show, and one of the contestants, a teenage girl who looked like she was thirty, had invited her mail man over as a guest to be in the audience. Apparently he'd heard her singing ever since she was a really little girl and there he was now in the audience. The camera didn't even zoom in on him so we couldn't see his face. We just saw the singer get vaguely emotional and then it was onto the next contestant. If we were brave enough to talk about these things to each other, we would need to talk about how brave we are, just to talk about these things.

All the packages are starting to pile up I worry what we'll do with all the boxes and how we'll have room to store all the items if none of it is ever used by anyone except me. I don't know if the aimlessness I've been sitting on and my lack of feeling any despair over it has to do with the fact that quite simply I believe this is the case for the vast majority of people in the world. I don't mean this in any condescending way since I do include myself in this group of the majority, this time I have to... I know I should feel a relief and I know I should be grateful because this new way of living is my gift, this new way of living is my way out somehow, too... Instead, I think what I keep sitting on, sitting without treading, treading while thinking, thinking of the cave five summers ago, is the idea that I could have actually done enough already, I may have already gotten enough actually. And I want to be clear I have not determined whether having done enough and having gotten enough are to be equated here, I know in many cases the usage or commingling of these things would be mistaken, but here, even in their disunity, there seems to be something shared. If I have gotten enough out of it, then there is no more I need to do. If I have gotten enough out of it, then it may become a point of despair were I to continue. If I have gotten enough out of it, then how could I not be aimless now? If I have done enough already, then does that mean I am still waiting for something? If I have done enough already, does that mean I must find something else to do? Until it has been done to the point of being enough as well? Instead I will make a plan to return to the cave this summer. A plan that doesn't keep. I must write to the keeper of the

house what appliances belong to the house already...
So that we might prepare what to bring ourselves. In
any event...

Day 38 / 8 at night

And how are the poets getting on these days? It's not
the question that sticks to me always but I want to
say I need to know and I am running out of patience.
I guess there are a million ways... Day job? Sugar
daddy? Swindle. But then I hear myself, I hear how
I ask and I hear how this drives all of the serious-
ness that I am bringing into this new community. We
literally swim in the news of the world but I can't
even muster up the business mind to write a column
for a voucher? What am I afraid of losing? Soon I
won't have a choice. What can I afford? The moment
of feeling washed over by microwaves, a useless
thought that can vanquish the empty news of the
world. Perhaps. If I can be happy, and by happy
I mean doing what I need and want to do, and yet
misunderstood by those around me, and yet causing
them to worry for me, can I continue? I now know
I cannot go beyond my dormancy without seeming to
those around me an utter failure a case of misery.

Can I discard this anxiety without discarding these relations?

I've put so much of myself out into the world, I have a thousand parts, parts of myself(.) S/seemingly in circulation(.) I/in the wakefulness of the world(./,) S/so I am bound to be disappointed each day! Even if I woke up one day, like tomorrow, today, and it didn't matter, matter that I would have to not be me in order to be understood by those around me, in order to not cause such worrying to those around me, what would I be worth? (

We can sit around for several hours and brainstorm how to make the most of what we've been given, what we've arrived at, and yet life continues to move us forward and so already more value has escaped. What I'm trying to say again is that a new way of living might be a form of running away and it might also be a form of a final straw. It's as if I've always known my stock value, now I can arrive at it, it's as if I've always known what would be sustainable, now I can understand why it's such a poverty, and why it's wrapped up in the future.

Why should I be so eager, for example, to bestow gifts when I have nothing, when I dwindle away? What abundance do I think I am even capable of latching onto, an abundance responsibly sourced from deep within? The other day, I thought of the sheets of song I had been collecting from the collection of the 'Dear Old Songs.' Are we the only ones? Of course not. In these pages I can sense clearly the old keepers of the same tunes I have heard so many times in my life while having some kind of clue of where they came from but not ever really being shown. At first I thought what a crime to cut these pages out, to cut these pages out and use them as envelopes. Quickly, without understanding why, I knew it was beyond acceptable. So I could have lived in one time, lived and been very useful. I could have lived right where I am, in that time, been so very useful, been even more afraid, a crime. So after assembling all of these envelopes, I was in the middle of doing something else when I remembered the storage room downstairs in the old home. All the old National Geographics kept there. Of course though I am not supposed to...

For a while, I had so many files open at any given time, so many. I would look at the files so often, I would open them so much, I got used to them. Blind. They didn't stress me out, they didn't distract me in the obvious sense. It was simply a part of my days, these files. I hadn't settled into the essence of my life yet. Maybe because it hadn't occurred to me that I had to really sacrifice anything in order to do so. Maybe I didn't even believe that one could settle into an essence, or... maybe a part of my youngest crime just knew that this idea of a singular essence was a lie itself and a half. I could not compare a before with an after because the thread was and is not moving in one direction. (..) Today once again I have many files open. After I'd spent the past few years trimming away, away, away, and realizing and realizing only to realize that that illusion of a singular essence was a lie, that that illusion was built on my fear of a single essence and the conspiracy of value and escape and sustenance. Still… at sometime, I befriended the illusion anyway, without a front, mind you, without one, and then… after being let in, I was informed that the front was exactly that, a front. The whole essence was a major decoy. A distraction. A sideshow. How I felt a sense of descent…

Today, however, I am afraid again. I am afraid and so I've spread out all the files again. The files that have always, in different forms, existed alongside, within, through, the illusion of essence. But maybe I gave them another way of speaking? It was only through speaking that I ever found a way to not be afraid of them. Because I know something that no one else, at least no one respectable, has ever shared personally with me, and I also know this something as something that is able to germinate in the debris. So maybe they, the respectable ones, also know but will not share, at least not with me. Why? Why? Because this I know, too, is something that these people, these beautiful, good people who have made it a gesture, who have made it a plea that has a simple answer, these people who ask for it in a way that is so put together, so put together when what they are saying is just the opposite of that, I know this is something that these people are actually afraid of. And I do not know how to approach. And I do not feel brave enough to ask. I have been told to stay back. All of us have. So I do. (")I've always wanted to see your ugliness.(") (")I guess I've shown you mine is all…(")

Is what we're doing playing house? Is the effort of a new way of living a more committed form of playing house? It all goes back to the house. The value of the house. The debt of the house. The people in the house. The garden behind the house (or in front). No, behind. The sink in the house The location of the house. The direction of the house. The correspondences and the paper work managed on behalf of the house. The community that meets in the living room of the house. A few years ago when we had the house to ourselves we put out a listing and it was easier than you'd expect to find lodgers who were interested in staying for a few nights, finding a crash pad, and then leaving. We learned many things, we had to, including plumbing. What the valves connected to, how to go into the furnace room to turn the pipes off, how to do it the old-fashion way. We also learned to not assume of human nature. Some of the coldest lodgers left the nicest words for us. Some of the warmest lodgers said nasty things. I've thought of how easy it all was or seemed even if it gave us migraines and we werer't nearly as equipped going into it as we thought we were.

So now that we have to find a new space to dedicate to our new way of living, it returns to the concept of a house.

Day 59 / 2 in the afternoon

I think about the community we are starting and I think about the other communities that have come before us and I think about the other communities that perhaps don't think of themselves as communities but which have things going for them I will be eager to take note from. And then there are the communities that have always had to think of themselves as communities, some of which I am learning I am less eager to take note from. Not that I am not interested in hearing their stories. I want to hear their stories but the reason I hear their stories is not because I think, what can we take from this into our own community? but almost more as a lesson, what do we want to make sure we do not take into our community? As I say this I am aware I may not be giving full credit to the goodness of these particular communities, I may not be taking into mind the reason for these particular communities to be, for example, over-sexed, starved for sex, overly casual with their sex. For there is nothing ungood about this. For I realize there is a certain level of privilege perhaps in my being distrustful now of the inebriated casual sex of certain communities. There is a certain level of privilege to have grown up around casually intertwined bodies, what someone recently told me is actually an orgy, and such. But intentionally, truly, we are not taking sex starvation into this new community nor are we taking a casualness with sex at all into our community nor are we taking inebriation into our community. Nor will those who are interested in joining the community yet who are starved for sex, who are overly casual with sex, who are inebriated, be shunned from our community. But these attributes will not form the fabric of our lives. There will be another type of casualness, there will be another type of inebriation, and certainly, we will not use the word revolution or revolutionary in any way, especially in a casual way. What to one community is considered radical, for example, this casual approach to intertwining bodies, this inebriated amory, to another community might come off as dishonest pageantry. What to one community is considered radical, for example, a distrust of this casual approach to intertwining bodies, a distrust of this inebriated amory, to another community might come off as dishonest pageantry. But this new community is made to recognize this and this new community is made to recognize this without any sort of hierarchy. I wonder how multiple communities can exist with each other and whether our community in particular will even be a singular community? I think not, and yet I do wonder at the same time... because maybe it feels that the pressure of this community will be such a way of pressure that if you were not to be a part of the community you would have no idea exactly what the demands of the community even were. But what will constitute being "a part" of the community? Am I to forgive or allow a certain approach to a way of life because I cannot possibly understand another community's identity, another community's background? I know forgive and allow is not the right way to think for I have not been slighted, I have been given nothing to take. Maybe the question is just, should I be open to whatever strikes me as too obvious in the way that they say priests would once remain in a forever too obvious state because of their avoidances but rather than allowing myself to confuse this form of avoided obviousness with the stately avoided obviousness, I just might recognize their similarities, I just might recognize their differences.

The closer we get to the beginning of our lives the more there is for us to prepare for. Rather than worry about it, I have let the lack of control be something that is in principal a good thing. If I am to see myself as a steward of the community, as both a leader and a lay person, which I do and am, then I will have to accept that there are some times where I will keep the community at the very front of my mind, some times where the decisions I make may seem to be entirely centered around what is best for the community, and that there are then other times where I will seemingly not have the community at the front of my mind at all, yet in that moment nonetheless, the community will still be on my mind, somehow, it will be on, in the back of my mind, present differently, where the decisions I might make seem not centered at all around what is best for the community but, more so, what is best for myself, what is best for someone who is either not a part of the community, does not even know that this community exists, or is truly a part of the community but doesn't yet know that they are. In any case, I am starting to see that preparing for the beginning of this community is to be at odds with many obligations that were begun before the complete formulation of the community could have even been entered into, and it is because it is at odds with these obligations that maybe this community is so important, and it is because it is at odds with these obligations that this community has a chance of being more than a thing, being both an idea and a thing.

I think about all the things that have had to happen in order for the idea of this community to have ever been brought into being. So much time. Yesterday, I was reading something that really had nothing to do with the community in one way, and yet in another way, it made me think of the all the people's work, all the work of the people, that must take place to make this community possible. All of the people's work, all the work of the people, that has taken place and all of the people's work that must continue to take place. There is the people's work of a type of community that for some people constitute the only community that matters perhaps and yet this type of people's work is both essential to the conception of our community, and yet it is not the only community within it either. There is the people's work of a certain type of performance or even production that occurs at the periphery, or at only one cross section, of our community. There is another people's work, too, of one or two people who partake in this performance or production going for a three or four hour ride to visit friends somewhere for one day only and this also constitutes an essential aspect, I think, of our community. And yet neither is this the essence of the community. It is not community's essence. And yet here I am still searching for clarity on this very matter.

Sometimes we have to be faced with exactly what we stand towards to recognize that there is anything to stand against. And I don't mean this in any holier-than-thou way. Could the one believe in me? I mean this in the way that sometimes we have to be faced with exactly what turns us off to recognize that we are not above being turned off by, by such and such. And not only that, feelings of disdain or distrust, which is it?, can cause a furry or fuzz of questions that make the necessity of this community, of what this community will serve, of what this community has always served, all the more real. Though this is not the moment where I will outline the building blocks of this community, I will however say that this community will not claim to serve as a safe haven for any particular group of people. It will not claim to do so ever. Because it cannot. It cannot. Neither will this community claim to even be a community once it has been fully formulated. It s best if no one knows that there is a community.

Day 62 / 1 in the afternoon

Have I always been this shy? I never recalled this before. Or discomforted by idleness? I guess so. Last night, on my way to bed, I felt this buzzing sensation in my chest. Maybe I never was able to feel it before, maybe it always buzzed? The one and I were facing away from each other in bed. We'd spent the past two hours fighting. I couldn't end the night that way. Even if I retreat into myself, I can't. I said as much. "I can recognize your flaws and my anger but I can still show affection. Why couldn't you? How could you be so cold? Way couldn't we hold each other still." The one thinks we'll forget about our anger, our flaws, and that then we'll move on from the fight too quickly. In a way, yes, I understand, I know. But it made my chest buzz and I didn't like that. Has affection always been my drug? We are trying to work through things. Be a happy couple.

Yesterday I missed the radical reproduction reading group. I was there on time but then I missed it. I joined the meeting but suddenly I got a buzzing sensation in my chest. Felt super shy and had to retreat away. I made up an excuse, I know, said the outage was coming up and left. I know. Even though all week it was what I was looking forward to so much, what I felt I was in need of. Same thing as today. Missed a call with an old friend because I got to getting shy. Maybe we were never that old. I read something the other day about someone finally having money at a certain point and it was a real benchmark that they could start seeing a therapist. I don't know when exactly that will happen for us but I think it's really something. Once we're there, once we're inside, we'll be ok, but it's the getting there that I get so worked up for. I'm so much in myself, in my own head. That's also my prize.

Before we left for the celebratory trip this weekend, I revealed to the one that sometimes I feel I am on the periphery of the community. "Why are we going then? How do you think I feel if you're on the periphery? So I'm the periphery of the periphery." But other times I feel like I have a right to be there just as much as anyone else. Really what it is is that I just prefer to be in the corner though I know what it's like to be cornered and to want to get out of that corner, still I know I would rather be in the corner with one or two people so long as no one feels like anyone there is being cornered, that we are just there together, catching up. With some people, it's like you don't see them in a long time and still you have a million things to say to one another and it's like the things you have to say kind of feel like, well, what have you been doing, what have I been doing, tell me, tell me everything, and like there's quite a lot to tell, or there's at least some, I don't know, story. With others, you almost skip straight through to the banter again and to the laughs again and to the quickness and to the being insouciant at the same time. So easy. Like you say everything that there is to say in just one heartbeat and then it's like nothing ever really happened, and it's like yesterday you were still together. I know all of us have different ways of showing our affection to each other. It's ok. It's ok. And then there are others you barely know though it feels like you could be the oldest of friends. No, that's not right... What's that? It feels like you could be very good friends, you could, but no, it'll never really happen, there's no time now, and you kind of know it always deep down but anyway it's all smiles and optimism and kindness and genuine interest, not pretend interest at all, mind you, not a gesture. And what do you do with that? Like something or someone's in the way? Anyway, with these people you skip the past because you aren't really close enough to get into those weeds but you don't exactly go into some old laughs or banter or easiness either. It goes into another space, a space of talking about the reasons you might do something, why you might, for example, want to be underneath the stars tonight, how hard it is to sleep with loud music playing even if the loud music is being generated by your old friends and even if you're wearing ear plugs, a space of telling stories to each other that have nothing specifically to do with this notion of catching up, for how could it, stories that I guess have more to do with getting to know each other, like sharing a part of ourselves. Do we sleep under the stars then? Tonight? When?

I could say that I've spent a lot of time thinking about what makes a particular community special, but I don't know if I ever really thought about it. I certainly felt it. Back when I felt it but didn't really think about it, maybe I was less on the periphery or maybe I felt less, I felt I was less on the periphery. Even if I was only a regular irregular. In a lot of ways I think I go further back with these central community members than some others. But it isn't the span of time that really matters. With this level of distance I can see that I am the one who is always reconnecting. I am the one. It does get tiring, this exercise of what? Avoiding the everyday dullness, avoiding the regularity of it? Deep down though I've always been with the dullness, I've always been precisely the regularity. But maybe either I sensed that my dullness wasn't sufficient for another's dullness, or maybe just because I mis-sensed my own need for deep regularity and dullness as being too out of character for the persona that I always carried as some spirit of reconnection. Maybe because of this the other always sensed a mismatch between the persona that I carried as this spirit of reconnection and the dullness and regularity of life in general. Or maybe what I think now is, too, completely wrong.

Maybe every single community needs people who go away for longer periods and then come back after an extended period of time to finally reconnect and then also the people, the ones, who are just regulars always. Maybe every single sustainable community needs people who go away periodically and then come back irregularly but also maybe they might need the people who will never leave, also might need the people who are there quite regularly for quite a while and then suddenly cause a lot of worry for everyone or they cause a lot of disappointment for everyone or they begin to show their true colors and it's then the community realizes that they could do without it or it's then the community stops being able to make excuses for it, these people. What do we offer besides a souvenir, I mean? Maybe my point in staying around in the afternoon and helping out in a practical way is my way of not allowing myself to just be a souvenir. To be someone who can show themselves in the dullness and the deep regularity of a community's ins and outs. (/) (()I thought I showed myself to be that kind of person years ago... ())(/) But maybe no one's ever even paid attention to that. And maybe it's too late now and I missed it long ago. Or maybe that's not really something anyone ever took the time to examine and assess. Like other things, it's just a given.

Day 64 / 10 in the morning

Within the greater community, there is a smaller unit of community. We are moving back and forth almost regularly between our fear that this smaller unit could be dire and the inconvenience of allowing this fear to crush this smaller unit. It isn't just the expectations of the community that we will soon become peripheral to, unbeknownst perhaps even to some of the key actors. (()But it will be my doing nonetheless.()) It isn't just the expectations of everyone involved either, everyone who we are putting on a show for, at all. There is a genuine reason to want to continue despite the reality that things could be. Mortality primarily. Besides, what do we mean when we say ruinous? Certainly many people have gotten themselves into much greater ruins and perhaps they would not think of it in such grave terms. Besides, greater's a bit dramatic, I'd think...

Was I always such a creature of comfort? Or am I on the same timeline as everyone else here and over there? Maybe all of us overtime have just become creatures of comfort anyway, maybe all of us wandering overtime just become creatures of comfort either way. The process of aging(,/-) maybe this is the act that invades us and makes it not only less convenient but also less sweet to thwart, to evade. We grow to rely on a convenience but through relying on a convenience do we convert? Do we cut ourselves off? There is something to be said about evasion. In that those who practice it as a way of living may be more forthcoming in their daily ins and outs, their everyday communication. Maybe something about the practice of a way of living of evasion allows that somehow? And conversely, I wonder if in my domestication, my perfecting of a life of domesticity and creaturely comforts, this stationary life, has made it so that I am less available to those I do not know, that I am less able to be candid, has made it so that my everyday communication with others is more forbidden, is more trying, is something I want to evade. And if this wanting to evade is a want that is more than I should want. We convert more knowingly with than we do without? Assuredly? Am I ready to lend a hand?

I am sitting on good news and I am also waiting for more news. The good news is never good enough, and any news at all takes years to come. Even as I hesitate to leap into the arms of a more stationary life, I await news to hear whether it will be possible for us to rest easy. Does anything actually get converted as a result of the news we could have received? We worry about the longterm viability of the conditions of our lives, I say we, when it's more just one of us, one of one, or one of two, I say it's more just one of us but maybe I just pretend and calm myself, calm myself down, because it's the only way to stay remotely manageable, to not completely dwindle away. Of course it is true it could be much worse, our always temporary rest, but who has that ever been a balm to? It is funny, I guess, to recognize that my belief that I made the right decision would be based on the fact that it has paid off somehow and to recognize yet also that I will never fully be able to explain this paying thing to others. There was no payment there. Even now I am fighting to prove that it was the right decision made. Each time more good news comes through the door, I am less ecstatic because I know that this perhaps adds only a bit more proof, proof that I made the right decision, adds more proof that my decision has paid off, and yet nothing has been paid off yet, it could only be the promise of something paying itself off still. I heard it(.) M/more or less.

It's the exact same part of myself that knows full well what to say in a group of people who form that very byzantine community of the most elect. What to say, kind of, or at least what not to say. It even happens with other communities that would never think of themselves as byzantine, and yet... And yet. Of course in this respect I am still learning. Like, who have I become unknowingly? Truthfully I cannot claim to have fully grasped this at all. Am I trying? I must be. Otherwise I would not be so occupied or quietly distressed about proofs at all. Anthropology. An-thro-po-lo-gy...

I can see the way she worries. It is a different worry than that of others around us who worry, who worry about other things, like putting on a show, and doing things according to some tradition or some sense of etiquette. I want to say, they are nothing alike. I want to say, they come from such completely different worlds. We have no idea how different the two of them are. So I see the way their worries are different. Those worries are mine as well, I mean, I have my own understanding of what is most important, though is it spoiled to say I am shouldering the worries of all of these ones, shouldering like trying to forge ahead at one single time? Forge ahead while getting nowhere, since the forging requires waiting? Waiting for news to come in. Like la violetera... or something. No... I don't want to get her waiting without warrant. In the past, too frequently I kept promising, I kept saying, wait wait wait, as I was telling myself to wait wait wait, too. In the past, in the past too frequently I said just wait, any day now, but nothing ever really changed. Even with the news. Sometimes, yes, there would be excellent news. But even then what did that excellent news do for our life? And besides, what do we want life to do for us all the time? She always said she wanted a simple life for us. She always said simple was good, simple was perfect. Now I want to hear her voice, and now I want to see her smile, but I know it is better for her to think one is busy, it is better to let her imagination wander... fill in the holes because then there's at least a chance that something better, better than just what's reality could be occurring. (/) Would I have preferred to have no waiting upon us now? Or would that have made me into a more despondent person somehow?

I wonder... about the life we want to live and... I wonder(...) about a life's reputation. The word optics comes to mind. And I wonder about asking for things, like... money. And I wonder about things like transparency and why it feels dirty sometimes to be wearing your needs so openly and why at other times it not only feels admirable, it feels like an act of recognizing life for what life is, it feels admirable for not apologizing for my needs either. Let's not pretend... Letters from prison about flowers? Ha! (   ) Ha! Is it brave or is it foolishness?

Is it goodness or is it admiration? Can these things be both and the same?

Day 67 / 430 in the afternoon

I think maybe I said the wrong thing, maybe I never spoke. But then I was always such a monogram. Now then they can't complain, not about me, not about me being too much of a monogram anymore. Too much of a diplomat. Whoever knew me knew I would never make it as a diplomat. I'd sooner be a diplomat's wife. Oops. What was that joke again? (")I wish...(")

Those little things that you have to navigate, it's not that there's not love there, but you realize everyone has to deal with them and you'd rather not deal with them here, you'd rather just be able to be alone with someone else, your person. Sometimes, when you're with someone who is your person, for example, and then, you're with someone who is your person's someone else, maybe your person's family, it's like you either don't feel you can be completely alone suddenly anymore or... you feel you have to put on a show again and it goes really bad, that's all. That's how it was for a while in the previous season for us and that's how it was too for a while in the

previous season for some of our dear ones as well.
Like, it's an unusual day, unusually hot, we feel our
dear ones moving on without us, but what are they
doing without us? W/we feel them going on to their
other lives, that's both our fault and theirs as well
though, and though we can't resent them for their
appetites, ultimately everyone has a problem.

For example, have I really taken over more as guide
or do I just feel less inebriated? Tonight I can't lie
I let myself go more. I had fun, I flirted with the
one's best friend's wife and I adored their child, I
did, I said flat out how eager it made me to have one
of my own. And then I thought of the everyday common
betrayal, the garage door opening, the toilet read-
justing itself, the plumbing, you never know who is
keeping something from you, you never know whoever
looks like they have their life together might just be
forging all the papers, and on the surface that's the
plan. That's how I feel today anyway.

She said she has a tear in her eye. Or. There's a
tear in her eye, she said. I can't remember now.
She was talking about the one… I can't remember
now. Something like that. It was… And now, yes,
the toilet's running. And the tooth has been flushed
down the toilet hole. Devilish. We're getting too far
down it. We're almost getting what we want. If we
can separate the mouth from the entire picture, but

we can't, but if we could, we could go into the most blurry mirror.

After a long day bouncing around the old city, old with rodent city, we want to come back to our own little town, our own little town where the rodents are more domestic maybe, and maybe not just roaming around wide open in the streets, after this, we want to have a place within our own little town to stay in, be at home too, not roam around. After a long day bouncing around the city, old with old friend city, city we have left for an indefinite time city and may have to leave for an even more indefinite amount of time, seeing some friends we used to see regularly, but not all, not the ones who are gone, and by regularly we of course only mean every month or two or so, for we were always homebodies, busy bodies, busy at home bodies(,/...) A/after a long day, we feel accomplished and we also feel we have so much to do at home now. It was hard to explain but I think we did a pretty good job of getting to the point of it, of explaining how there was a moment last season when we considered catching the big move, deciding to leave more permanently, but we weren't quite there and then we missed that wave, how we still consider making the big move if we were to catch another wave, but we aren't sure whether that big move could in any way be a big move back or just a big move elsewhere, how close or how far, or how truthfully everything, misfortune aside, has made me see how narrowly we had been spending ourselves before, how narrowly we had been living for so long, how our attachment to a place was really so frivolous, how much space we had been invisible to, how much space had been invisible to us, how so much is still as we speak actively converting and yet it's odd because we've seen how quickly we left a new old city, we've seen how hurriedly we just left a new old city blank, left a city wide behind, and how we were fine anyway, and the world around us actually opened up they say, news closed out the world somehow opened up? A/and so then we feel it, we feel if and when the time comes for us to move again, whether back or elsewhere again, we can do it, we can do it even with no time. And they understood. They just did. I felt like I wasn't making any sense but somehow I made complete sense to them. Oh well.

Being back there again by ourselves for the first time in what was just one revolution made me effervescent in a way and I couldn't tell either if it was a new effervescence or if it was a fully ripened effervescence. How could I stare long enough at the other people picnicking with their friends in the park to really figure out whether the effervescence I sensed peripherally from those others around was a genuine effervescence or if it was affected, if it was a genuine effervescence that was at ease with its own despondency or if it was an affected effervescence that felt like it would do anything to get rid of something despondent within it. I couldn't tell, I stole glances here and there but I couldn't stare long enough, I wonder though.

Is it a sign of something that it is less enticing to me to imagine from the vantage point of another center, with me as the periphery, or of another periphery, with me as the center, is it a sign of something that this is less enticing to me than it is to ask for example what is the difference between the lives of a group of people in a specific age group, the lives of a group of people who are for the most part coupled off anyway, childless, people who frequent parks together, who picnic together in parks together, in parks in a specific neighborhood with a specific demographic of income, class, age, the difference between the lives of this group of people and the lives of another group of people, also coupled off, also frequenting parks, but doing so differently, that is to say, doing so with offspring, doing so on a slightly different schedule that of course revolves around the sleeping and feeding habits of such offspring, and so doing so at a different pace, doing so at a different level of organization, doing so with different expectations, doing so with a different kind of contentment? Is it?

I think I'm starting to realize it's not about the park and it's not about the location of the park. We could in a way walk through any park, set up a blanket in any park, whether we were one type of couple or another type of couple. We could, but someone on our periphery, someone whose periphery we belong to, might see us one way or another. And maybe how much we choose to engage with those on our periphery, those whose peripheries we belong to, and by engage I mean stare into, stare after, engage with, or how much we choose to be lost in ourselves, to keep the periphery purposefully blurry, maybe how much of this will dictate what desires form of all the other players around us on any given day. It's impossible perhaps for it not to.

Day 10 / 9 in the evening

How hard was it to pass the test? Very hard. I guess I have to start from the beginning but I don't want to lose hope so easily. Starting from the beginning feels like whatever the opposite of remission might be, whatever deadlock. For a while I was moving forward, forward, forward, but I was also standing still, but I was running in place actually. The one who has threatened to be my whole world, the one to make community with me, mentioned how all this forwardness was really just a way to not stay still, which is ironic, since I was trying to stay as still as one possibly could, I was trying my hardest to stay as still as is possible for one. which is how I ended up going forward and effectively defeated the whole purpose of staying still at all. Anyway this one had mentioned how all that forwardness made it impossible for me to hear my own thoughts. I thought that was very apt. But it didn't scare me enough. I kept going on with it.

Now life has taken another course. It's funny how you can be so hung up on doing things one way, on saying "No."... and knowing your reasons for doing so, too, and then, when given the opportunity, you start placating everyone around you without realizing you're accidentally placating them, even though your whole reason for saying no wasn't to not placate them exactly, it's actually the accidentally placating them that ever made you realize why you said no in the first place, not to not placate them but because you had your own reasons for saying no that apparently responded to those people's reasons for saying yes if they'd ever happen to be in your shoes. It's funny... how now that you're doing everything you said you wouldn't do, you're doing it really well and time marches, time is marching forward and the weeks have gone by and no real news has happened except the national news, except the news of names.

I'm not touched. When I say this, I don't mean this sarcastically in the way I may have once meant it ironically. Or, hey, lovely idea. I say it as in the moment, I actually thought, hey, I'm not touched. Even if it could be untruthful, it's not insincere. For example, earlier today, I was catching up on some old news. Stupid idea I guess but I really started feeling like it was the only thing that could keep me accountable. Perfect merging of the news of the nation and the news of another local community that has global participants. There were certain moments when I did cry. But I didn't weep, no. I started to cry but then old news kept pouring out, news and commentary, and then I kind of shrank away from the moment of crying. So when I said, I'm not touched, I mean I glossed over the fact that there apparently was something being touched, and yet I would not describe exactly the touching as a state of endurance, not that endurance is static or anything. Not that I do not endure.

I'm half-heartedly trying however to figure out what grappling with the course even means for us right now. How could I speak for all of us? It's possible this is what they mean by not having enough time for certain things. I admit I never really understood what that meant only because I did not see time as an obstacle more than an excuse. If you care, you make time for it. Simple. But I'm seeing now that that one hundred percent is what gives time away. That one hundred percent so split.

The word reconciliation scares me, too, though it came to my mind just now when I thought maybe there is some secret point of reconciliation between what I was trying to do here anyway and how I have already gone off course. If it's so hard to say goodbye, why is it so hard to keep in touch? A part of me wants to just say that this was the part that wasn't a part of the plan that probably always should have been a part of the plan. Since part of the trying was to consider a way of living. Not in a lofty sense. Not Thoreau. It was almost more to consider whether considering a way of living could even be done with any meaning. What is ironic is the living I was considering considering, in pure description, would seem very different from the living I am making plans for right now. Yes(,) I have many plans for a living I may not tell. But why shouldn't I tell about them? Not because they aren't enticing but because I am afraid I have not done my job in explaining why I should be forgiven. For example, in the process of making all of these plans, I have had to learn many things I never knew about. It's not those things in and of themselves that save me, it's that they provide some kind of sustenance to this entire trying. This project. Already now I start thinking how this will end up being a sinister aspect but because I anticipate this I am also inclined now to say hey... don't think so much about it.

For example, I want to tell you how this week I have been speaking with a press woman about a set of laser engravings on wood. We have just exchanged several letters even though when I said that it sounds like I went into the store on main street and spoke to a woman at her store. Actually I spent an entire forty eight hours just considering dimensions of wood paper engravings and the number of holes I would need die cut into these wood paper engravings and how I would ultimately attach these wood paper engravings into corked moss. Did I enjoy this? Was this necessary? When I set out to do something and I have a motive, it's hard to be rational at all. At a certain point, it becomes the only thing that matters to me.

What I enjoyed about this woman was her energy and warmth. I told her that. Almost as much. I couldn't afford this woman but I wanted to make it work with this woman. She just riffed with me and made me feel like my idea was something worth getting excited about. She seemed genuine. I guess I've acquired a way for knowing when someone seems genuine or not, made easy because I believe no one would take the time to counterfeit enthusiasm in this day and age. Besides, there is some enthusiasm that can't be counterfeit. The enthusiasm that takes time and caloric intake and conversion. That's what she gave me, enthusiasm that takes more time than most, more time than even counterfeit. It was this enthusiasm that made me start thinking irrationally. It's funny... because this whole project feels like both the most rational thing I've ever done and also the least business-minded. Funny to think I've somehow been business-minded this whole time at all. What a joke.

Are the voices of all these other people leaving me or are they just fully settled and absorbed in me? Are they my friends? Does it matter if I think of them as friends?

Day 2 / 2 in the afternoon

Now that I am no longer outlining the terms of this treatment, or now that I am not at the very beginning of outlining the terms of this treatment, it's kind of like getting showered up in the morning, putting shoes on, getting ready for a new job that after day one is already no longer zesty, attesting to one's serious need for patience. For what we are setting out on does not stand in direct opposition to what I set upon myself, hardly, nor is it nearly as weighty as one might initially think when confronted with (") a new way of living.(") For I have learned... I have learned that there is the nostalgia of thinking of the less recent past as though it were from a purer time, as though the people who lived in it were a purer people, as though their deals were purer, as though what they were capable of was still purer. And then there is the nostalgia of the more recent past as though that too somehow surprised us with its purity, surprised us when we thought such community was no longer even possible in our own era, when we thought all community was hostility.. in our own era. And then... you get to the nostalgia for the very now as well. I do not know which one to be more suspect of. I want to say that's not the way to go about it, to side with one suspicion.

It's also true that there is a connector between these three different nostalgias that has nothing to do with suspicion, that has no business at all with suspicion. (It's also true that there are many, many more than just three different nostalgias but for the purposes of this explanation three should suffice.) Like, different forms of consciousness don't have to be leveled up and it's hard to be critical of the delicate community who also read and write their own cave poems for each other when all they want to do is write their own letters to each other. I guess it's the earnestness that bends me, the earnestness I want to believe, the earnestness I have seen the face of too and yet I encounter now as wearing wholly another face, the earnestness that has proven to be no friend of mine. A contraption(!) Sincerely I am out of it today.

So this is my first test to commit myself to the constancy of the project which really isn't a project but more so, yes, a way of living. As already given, perhaps I will just float between project and way of living for a little while in order to avoid the gravity that comes with way of living and in order to avoid the obvious supply-chain that comes with project management. It makes sense to not wholly let myself be consumed for starters. I could perhaps prevent this—the being fully consumed—by referring to the treatment as a kind of project or as a new way of living. Both of these could balance each other out ultimately and both of them could balance out me as well. One thing that might be helpful as I embark upon this project, or rather, way of living, is to just outline the exigencies of the moment. A lot is taking shape right now, for example, a lot of stones are being placed and placed down that is. We move from fully unbolted into a leap of faith practically overnight. Is it leap of faith or is it pragmatism? Is the Sunday market a leap of faith or is the Sunday market pragmatism? Is the Sunday paper a habit or is it a rem(a)inder?

It is hard to describe the exigencies of the moment as it is hard to stand by the description of what needs to be described as the exigencies of the moment. I think what I mean by this is that it feels like we have not much time left. Like, for example, I want to do certain things, there are still certain things that… and there are certain things that have nothing to do with these desires, nothing that seems needed to be done if I am to do those things I want. Compromise keeps coming up more frequently but in actuality it feels much worse than that. What is worse than compromise? It is not a negotiation but the borderline of rationalization. We would have to commit so fully to this new way of living and, even then, it would be no one's fault.

I didn't mean to be dramatic when I invoked time and temper. Some things, it is true, like friendship, cannot be quantified. If you asked me this question two years ago, I would have certainly answered completely differently, not an answer in direct opposition but the formulation of the answer would have been so foreign to now. Is saying that I feel I have not much time left really the same as saying I am making good time but in order to continue I have to make some tough calls now, I have to set some stones down? It seems like this could still go the way we want it to but we have to do all we can to not become clouded up.

Someone said something today that wasn't totally striking but now I think back to the image of a cloud that has absorbed all of water and is just sitting there now above us, ready to strike. How did this weighty thing which holds all the rain become so innocuous and gauzy? And how did this thing that is so innocuous and gauzy become a way to describe what it feels like to be confused? There are a few ways to interpret this and I have to seek the fullness and actuality more now. I'll burst...

Remember when I mentioned the narrative of the one who is swept away and the one who sweeps? It isn't my intention to make this a running thread. All I'm trying to say is that even though it would really be plain cheap to compare the two of them with the two of us, it is useful for me to see why my mind keeps going back and back to it. On the inside, it's really easy to justify this and to justify that and to rationalize it all away, to say I got this, so I'll give that up, like, what's really important to me is this, so saying ok to that won't really matter, will it? On the outside, would I see someone just making up excuses, someone who should really know better?

I don't ask a lot of this project, this new way of life. By asking a lot we can accidentally go in the exact direction we were trying to steer away from. It is hard for me to prevent the immediate build up of expectations but that is what I'll have to do. Because it is another trap. The trap of setting out the intention of, for example, the intentional community on the outskirts of the central community but which also participates in things more centrally located within that community, for example, when it is needed to stir things up or procure particular goods that cannot from within be procured outside of the community on the outskirts, there is the trap of setting out such an intention and actually becoming very good at this one way of living, and then finding that a lot of time was swept away as well, and that though time being swept away may not be naturally bad, who said it ever was, still maybe you will only have gone this way to say that's what you do, still maybe you will only have gone this way because it is simpler and it doesn't make you not happy after all and you will have played your part. So what?

Well, perhaps playing my part is the problem.

Day 24 / ?

Maybe the change I began to see in me was the revolution I stopped thinking about. Who am I accountable to? Why do I draw pictures of animal constellations? Is the clinging to of animals a sign of naivety as a personality of character or a sign of the revolution carved out of fairy tales? It has been six weeks or more of me finding something that I was naturally good at that wasn't the training speaking and I started seeing how it could all go one way—tree, house, mailbox, etc. It has been 36 hours of trying to draw pictures of animal constellations, to say that I tried and I don't think I'm doing anything wrong because we can't have it any other way. Now we know. Only now. Now I'm willing to make myself culpable. I have to count my losses and assess the risk. Respect. I haven't been keeping up with training but more and more I know as well in a way that the training never taught me—respect. Similarly, what exactly I've been up to these days could also never give me what all the years of training once and for a long time did.

I'm trying to gain back time. While knowing full well it is gone and being ok with that. No one wants to be friends with a middle one who feels exactly her middling anyway, one wants to be friends with a middle one who feels a lot younger and older at the same time, that's all, full stop. So should I not be insulted when I hear, you could be very young or you could be very old. Should I be? I should be I guess, or I've been told, but I'm not. I won't. But you can't plan which one you'll become, can you? Now there's the rub, you can't plan which one you'll become otherwise your plans would likely be thwarted anyway. If it took me this many years to get nowhere, I have nothing to worry for where I've been the last few months. I found it charming as well that the one thought I had been productive. What a funny way of putting what I've been doing.

Adding new items to the basket, adding new items to the list, crossing off items to the list, taking items out of the basket, some new items being things, other new items being actions that require the procuring of things. When I say I noticed myself being more transparent the other day when I said To sharing blackberries in the valley ahead soon... I realize now that that transparency was reserved for some people, not for every, it remains a reserved transparency, and maybe even transparency isn't the right way to say it. Boom—a flash.

(

)

We are paying all of what we, in the new community, saved in order for me to be closer to the people who most likely won't even be around after the station. We are paying dearly for it but we know it is the best solution and mostly I know nothing lasts forever. What's the point of holding onto all of our savings anyway, it's not like we left behind everything simply to stay, I have gotten something out of being here that I never anticipated. Could we get something out of being elsewhere, on station, again? When people say it "looks good on her," what do they even mean, have they really thought it through, I think not. Just now when I was finishing up a chore that was a reminder that chores are why I am alive, I thought, if I could encapsulate a day, each day, for a month, that would also suffice to be a project worthy of being done, but this is not my project, my project is perhaps precisely to resist such a project. This is my project.

Like, do I want to show-off to everybody and say look look what I can do, because I could do that ostensibly without making it seem obvious that what I'm trying to do is give a great performance, because after all, any thing I do is my most honest side in the moment. Like, I could show my years of training, and I could show how detached I can get or go. Or, I could trick them without really meaning to. I could leave that space and be utterly misunderstood, that is to say, maybe people won't get the purpose of the project and instead they'll just attack it for not being showy enough. This is what I fear, this is what happened already, that the lack of showmanship will come back again as an issue. That is, keep me awake at night with petty thoughts. Then it keeps me honest...

So then again I think the people who this is made for, those who I have in mind, and those who I am yet to know we have this connection, will understand.

Day 39 / 4 in the afternoon

I started doing really simple things again. If I were positioned one way I would just shift ever so slightly and see if I felt anything another way. I used to do this too but when I made the shift I would feel something immediately, a crack in the bones, for example maybe, and I would think, oh... I need to be softer to my body, oh.(..) Now when I make the shift I don't hear anything, no crack or anything, and surprisingly, somehow I am more alarmed, somehow I feel even worse, somehow... It's like a more enveloping ache that won't even offer any loosening. I wanted to tell about this in the way I imagine people telling in their writing of letters to their family across the main line back in the 70s when they first started discovering this new thing called yoga. Talking about the mysterious ways they found new spaces inside their bodies. If I heard someone talking now, talking seriously, about their yoga helping them find new space, if I heard that today, there's a fifty fifty chance I would take what I could get out of it, the therapy, let's say, and discard the rest. Probably I went a little too hard myself when I lived across the main line right after my hey day and did more than my fair share of dabbling in yoga, too. Probably...

Today I feel like a living breathing art work. Can I say that? I feel that way and I know I am and I know that I have no price tag and that makes me disappointed. What's the point of being a living breathing piece of art if no one can buy you, steal you, work out a heist and get the whole system seeking after you, notify all the authorities that you're missing, be so precious that you're the only bargaining chip for some criminal? World class, no less. There's no system to verify if it's an original or a forgery. I'm a useless living breathing work of art.

So I figured I should try, I figured the best way was to just walk down the street of the main part of town, see what didn't totally discomfort me, walk in and ask, are you hiring? Now, as you can imagine, is a terrible time to do this. So rather than them asking me, can you roll your sleeves up, can you stand for several hours non-stop, can you carry up to 50 pounds of boxes? It was me saying I can roll up my sleeves, I can stand for several hours non-stop, I can carry up to 50 pounds. But it doesn't work that way. Still I had to say something. Our plan relies on me saying something when I go into a store on main street. It's a new kind of putting myself out there. We were sitting outside on the deck on a foldable table and two foldable chairs having lunch today. I was eating meal right out of the plastic container, no plate, no cutlery, one flavored pancake and another flavored pancake with dried syrup. It was the most luxurious thing we had in months. I was tired but I could fight but not energetically so I was calm and asked questions. That's how I get.

On a day like this... On a day like this where it is not sunny but it's gorgeous to be outside, it feels gorgeous, it's not a pretty sight, but no one's watching today, so we're out on the deck, and it's not sunny so no one's watching today, and you feel the oil on you and the dandruff and the plaque and your sturdy legs like voila (—) so it feels gorgeous. You even have time to notice how lush the surroundings are now and you notice the surroundings more because it is not the most beautiful day sight-wise. It is beautiful in another way. So maybe lush is wrong. So maybe lush isn't about being lush, not about being lush each on their own or not about making lush with lush. It's a lush of deterioration, a secret lush in the make-believe. And we keep going back and forth, we both know each of us harbors doubts but what about? the old saying we took with us? I say I am less afraid of real escape but that's not true. I say I am less afraid of losing the investment but that's not true. I am more afraid of what it means to be flippant over the investment than the chance of escape.

Day 57 / 3 in the afternoon

We are less than four weeks out from the move and big news arrived yesterday. (We made it, we got the chance, and we decided to go ahead.) I was finally put through to my mother and all we could talk about was the fall and our progress on everything and we sent each other updates and I told her to not be hurt that none of her children sent her gifts for Mother's Day, it's a sign of the times, we all would have tried if we could, and I did not think how spoiled, we commiserated, we both said, life is short, and then I said I should be going, I have to keep getting ready for the fall, I have to go now and we both said love and hung up. Just like that. A minute later I opened the letter to the big news. I ran to tell the one and then I tried to reach my mother and let her know. Miraculously, I was put through and I could tell from the sound of her voice she heard good news in my voice. So I let her know and then we had a walk down memory lane together, very quickly, like vroom vroom vroom, because even with good news, there was no time to actually stop, have a drink, a cold drink together, a warm drink together, celebrate, no, I had to keep going... Did I forget to celebrate?

I think the big news couldn't have come at a better time. It was a reminder to me of all that's moved. I didn't even have time to put my feet up and really celebrate, I still haven't and maybe won't ever get to it. Maybe I am celebrating right now. Why is there something comforting in recognizing I couldn't put my feet up at big news, I couldn't even celebrate? Is it because there is something comforting in recognizing time passing, time moving? I do not feel afraid of that now.

Yesterday marked the beginning of a big new chapter and the closing of a smaller chapter. How can we ceremonialize this? Is this what I want? To ceremonialize?

I never had a desire to be a part of an opening, like a restaurant. Just like I never really had a desire to do x y or z. Not the way I have a desire to join the community. Stay in the community. Not the way I have a desire to make food for us, to make food that makes one and one smile. I never had a desire to make a code. But I have maybe been more and more in that mindset these days. Maybe I'm on the cusp from putting a deposit down, on the cusp of putting something we don't have down, something either frivolous or truly invaluable.

The day got a way from me again. I'm not too guilty feeling though. The other day I went to the mail office and sent off a straggled letter. The last one I guess. As well as a package for returns. Later that day I packed sandwiches and did final checks on everything. Then we were off. Only one major refuel stop along the way. And only one major fight. We managed.

Before today I was not worried about rejoining the community. I really wasn't. A part of me almost felt bad that I was enthusiastic, even when speaking to my closest friends in the community, I thought, is it ok if I show this enthusiasm? But I really can't wait, if I'm honest about it. Still, today, I would be lying if I said I am now worried. I only know we will have more obstacles than I had originally thought we would have. But again, as I said, more obstacles could actually only be more fortifying. More obstacles could mean we have to figure out a way in, which is better than just sitting where we are, wherever we are, and not figuring out a way at all, and is better than waiting for the way to show itself to us. Being aimless is no joke because it is no longer a choice, it's a reason. And I almost forgot there would be other people involved. Not literally, not literally involved, but the consequences of what it means that there are other people involved and that other people are also figuring out how to rejoin the community. Say hi. Say how are you. Get in.

By all accounts we are on schedule. The past few days have gone as planned. This was a big part in our transition back into the community even if it seems totally beside it. Making it through these past few days is no small feat. Again, no celebration, no, we have not celebrated, not really. Yet almost all of our meetings were kept, all of our errands were completed, all of the major tasks we had set for ourselves to complete have been completed. Now there is just the work of really getting in touch with the community members. One on one, one by one, setting aside time with ourselves to followup with the community members, setting aside to listen to the community members. I don't even know how this will happen yet. Actually, as I say this, I am realizing this is part of my lesson. The fact that it is so trying for me to know how to followup with the community members. I have always found there to be something most meaningful in the avoidance of the obstacle and surely this can be no different? I am falling more and more behind on this. This is the one thing we seem to be falling behind on. I think this is the lesson.

And why is it so hard for me to followup with the community members? What has been missing in my life? I guess I have never really been a part of the community. Even now, I am noticing how I want desperately to be a part of the community and yet simultaneously it's so hard to really figure it out as I go, as a fellow community member, it is so hard to know if I have only ever been beside, on the periphery. So maybe it's the fellow-ness I am uncertain of. How fellow could I be to them? Do they view me as being a mere fellow evaluating them? I am though. I am both evaluating them and I am a community member. There's no way around this.

People are very busy these days. I can feel it. I am too. I wonder if I am rushing through everything. Following up with the community members is definitely something I don't want to rush through. Other things you can rush through. But not that. It would be too damaging to our entire aura and I believe it would create a chain reaction I don't want to have to deal with. Make me extremely paranoid and such. Or, make me much more extremely paranoid than I already am, and such. That is, make me aware of my paranoia.

It's not that it seemed promising before and that now it's not promising. I know what makes something a promise is only as much as what I am willing to give back to what I get. So I can't be so discouraged or make these excuses. My expectations will be what gets the best of me here. If my intentions were to roll my sleeves up and get my elbows a little greasy, now seems to be the chance to say so. Bored was not so bad but being bored here will be the thing to get you killed.

Day 69 / 10 in the evening

One went into town yesterday morning before we went into the city. One wouldn't tell me exactly why but I knew. When I questioned one about it, one admitted to me the reason and then one asked if I wanted to come next time. I said I would think about it and then I said, no, you go alone. Not because I didn't want to be involved in the decision making but because I wanted one to handle this one thing without me, and also I wanted that hour of time to myself, even if I wasn't going to do anything important with it, it was my choice to do nothing with an extra hour to and for myself. Everything being so rushed these days, as we get ready to go... Trying to check things off a list one by one these days. So one went by oneself into town and then one came back with pictures. On our way into the city I looked through them and told one

to stay to the left and then stay to the right and
then continue for five or six miles and look for exit 9
and soon along our ride I felt my head spinning and
needed to close my eyes and not hear one talking at
all. I remembered the old trick of looking far enough
way at the edge of the horizon until you found some-
thing that was always constant even while you were
moving. It helped.

I really mean it when I say what we are doing is
simply to please people around us, people who mean
a lot to us, and so we are doing this for something
called mortality. These people, they care. Things
that don't necessarily mean so much to us mean
something to them, and since it doesn't bother us so
much to please them on this matter, there's no point
in fighting it, we might as well give them what they
want. But giving them what they want is also tricky,
isn't it? At some point we also decided that if we're
going to do something to please people around us,
we're going to please people around us our way then,
our own way. We keep saying that, we keep saying,
we're doing it our way, we know how to do this, we
only know how to do this our own way, we will only
compromise so far, we will give them what they want
but we will make them regret wanting it. It's hard
to know how much of it's really us at this point, how
much of it is really any different from the way these
other people would do it themselves anyway. So maybe

we can meet each other in the middle. Maybe we can meet in the middle and make ourselves regret ever doing this either way.

And then there are the little details I never imagined myself caring so much about and yet somehow they make for great fun, they take advantage of me, and are even appreciated eventually. In turn, I appreciate their appreciation. These little details corner me and I realize they dress up a life. I am neither entirely a dressed up wall nor am I an entirely empty one. I could be either, I wish I could just be empty. I could be either but instead I notice the smudge marks, I zero in on them, and they call me to cover them. So I go into town, spend a day or a half a day there, picking up things along the way, things discarded and things left behind, things I might be able to cover up the smudges with, and then end up piling them into the play room anyway, because it takes me months to get the proper supplies, the nails, the hangers, to even put the pieces up.

Being back in the neighborhood was like viewing the results of an overly hyped up case study that we were not particularly interested in learning about. And yet we were two of the specimens adding to the data. Anyway, we caught up with some old friends whose demeanors had not changed at all, at least not in any way detectable. We used the restroom,

we plugged ourselves in, and we were too flustered
to allow the mess of t all to bother us beyond a
level of judgment. Before seeing our old friends
again, as time has continued moving forward, our
understanding of them had been becoming more and
more perhaps like cardboard. And then seeing them
again took us into the scented again in a way that
relies on the past to show it what it would be other-
wise. The being flustered of it helped keep us in
the present moment, the being flustered helped keep
us up to speed. As someone mentioned, it was the
most city-like encounter in a way. Birthday party,
running errands, visiting friends with baby, going
over contract, meanwhile we're parked in the wrong
place and trying to take apart this piece of furniture.
Someone who is constantly running around, ostensibly
busy, seemed to think we had a very productive day,
but to us, what did we even do, we were so tired, we
had a great day, and what did we even do?

We had always held our old neighborhood up as an
example and as a reason to be afraid of ever leaving
our old neighborhood. We had always held up our home,
which was never ours, as an example, too, but anyone
could tell you that our situation was unlikely because
we just happened upon it for reasons that are totally
impossible to plan. But if the past year has proven
to us anything it's that there was no reason for us
to be afraid of leaving. And now, going back, as

released specimens, as people who are shown the polished brochure of the case study results, we could see why it would be impossible for us to ever go back maybe. We could maybe even one day view our time there as an era that may have never been given the bookend to become an era had we not been faced with the unfortunate circumstance of having to leave in a hurry. It's hard to understand how I can allow myself to go back. Well, because I need one, and one needs me, and one's community, however fractured, is still holding on in the city. We did this to ourselves.

I've tried to explain to one the importance of sending oneself forward, no matter where you are. It's very easy actually. If you aren't familiar with this idea, you may need to close your eyes. But if you've been doing it for a while, it's something you can practice anywhere, even while you're looking someone else dead in the eyes, even if you're looking someone dead in the eyes and listening to them talking, meanwhile you're away, sending yourself forward. It's important, I said to one, try to think of how you'll feel, how you'll smell, what the space will smell like, to imagine the space around you, the people around you. Otherwise, you're going on half-knowledge. Otherwise you haven't done everything you could have done to really paint a picture and inevitably you'll have made the wrong decision then.

Last night, the top of the headboard got too close to the wall and started shaking against it and making a knocking sound and in my sleep I thought someone was knocking on the door. I was too tired to do anything about it or I was too tired and I also knew subconsciously there wasn't really a way for me to handle the situation properly so I stayed half-sleeping but then meanwhile was also aware that all of us could be coming under attack from wanderers. It made sense to me that if you were going to attack us, you would first knock loudly, several times, to see if anyone would answer, and that's as far as I needed to go to think that someone could be trying to gain in on us. In my half-sleeping of course I didn't stop to think that we had vehicles on the driveway or what time it was. All I know is that by the time I was up because it was too cold and the fan was blowing directly on me and I needed another cover, we had survived, no one from the other family on the other side of the house had screamed, so it must have been the headboard, a suspicion I had already begun to feel when I dozed off again completely.

Day 1 / 9 in the evening

What are my expectations for this new way of living? I guess I could begin pragmatically. First I have to remark that the units aren't particularly large, I want to say they're actually quite small, not too variable, at most a few heads, but often just two. If I begin to speak about heads, I think of the main state's placement against the rest. I promise I had no intentions with this new way of living except one possible formula which I intend to keep to myself for as long as possible. Not to maintain some mystery, but because perhaps it will be a way to keep just one thing for myself, as in, everything else I hope might be revealed over the course of this exercise. So this thing kept will effectively be the variable, the constant, around which everything else might be sustained.

When I originally mentioned heads, I wasn't talking strictly about heads around a table, although if I am to be honest, it's been on my mind, conscious and otherwise. Then when I said it, it felt like the only word that could be used, and once I committed to it, the main state arrved. It may be worth saying, no more mention of the main state, it may be worth setting myself off by prohibiting any references from here on out. I always thought I lived in an alternate universe. Actually I lived very far in an alternate universe, danced all around it, came back simultaneously both more in my own head and indestructible and much scarier and less afraid, but like in a good way and became another caricature. Then fast forward some odd years. But really, I thought even recently, this was the alternate universe.

What do I mean by this? I guess that there wasn't a whole lot of unfortunate second-guessing, only fortunate second-guessing. Like, somehow I really thought we were on the outskirts, not that we aren't, not that we aren't on the outskirts now, because in some ways, this is about as out of the outskirts as we could have gone, and yet in other ways, I guess I realized it's just dull as well. And don't I want a dull life? Isn't that all one could hope for? A dull vibrancy? Which I guess brings me back to the old point. I am not specifically charged here with logging a specific time of day, a specific year, or even some utopic possibility of life. I remain as distrustful of the community as ever, I mean even the community of the outskirts, because I have fallen for it so many

times, in its different forms, before. And I do not
say this out of defense. I do not say I have come a
long way. I do not say I can see their world from
where I sit, like fanning myself or something, that's
not it at all. It is painful for me to do anything
besides the chores these days, besides keeping track
of items, besides putting things in the basket and
taking things out of it.

I am not specifically charged with capturing. There
was great pain and pleasure, though, in my experi‑
ences of other people's capturing, this I can say and
stand by because I feel it still when I say it. For
example, one of them began almost casually. Like two
people meeting, for example. And like one of them is
proverbially swept away. And like the other one is
the one we don't really like because they're a little
too aggressive and maybe even abusive but is the one
charged with doing the sweeping away. But here's the
thing, I want to say this wasn't set up. It has to be
set up is what we think because it's so casual and
it's how casual it is that leaves us so unprepared for
that late unraveling moment when the one swept away
will eventually stand still like her legs are basically
held down by weights, like she's basically a statue in
a park, a statue that people just walk by and don't
really ask many questions about because it's insig‑
nificant enough and not especially obtrusive either.
So the origin is very casual. It is an origin. The

origin is a basic set up. And a kind of life rolled out of that. One that could be pretty much related to, in the sense that this life occupied the real world for a certain time or period of history. I think also it was spoken of as though occurring in the past but with the emotion of the present or maybe it was spoken of as though occurring in the present but with the emotion of the past yet avoided any bit of nostalgia. It was in the most painful moments actually that the nostalgia arrived? And that's what made it acceptable. Because basically they had nothing, they were poor, the one swept away and the abuser who did the sweeping, like somehow they were both caricatures and real people at the same time, like someone you know everything about and at the same time you don't know some things really important about but you could fill in your own ideas nonetheless. They were poor and, as a result, irresponsible.

I'll never forget when I first encountered this feeling. (/) And when exactly I was feeling so exhausted, like so exposed, and so out of touch with the purest parts of me, I suddenly realized the loop began again. Because all it took was this assignment basically. All it took was this assignment of starting this new way of living and then that feeling of exhaustion, exposure, being out of touch, became an offering. Not useful. An offering. Like rather than assessing myself and leaving it at that I could offer my assessments not into the creation of something but into a way of being. But not a way of being that was at all apart from the real world. Not a way of being that was utopic. Anyway it would either stick or it wouldn't. Anyway it would come back to me eventually once the new way of life became old and it was time to put it away in a drawer or give it away as an offering itself.

It's hard to discern whether we gave each other aches or just an alternate universe of brain chemicals or if it's everyone else who just made the call. In a split second I went from being wary, very wary, not sure if I could continue not sure if I could continue without pulling my hair out, to thinking, hey what if I reached out and said, hey I think this was meant to be. Now that I'm lukewarm I realize it's clear I'm the one with all the brain chemicals going like this, going like that... After all, though I might sometimes slip into a register, a feeling, that recalls a 19th century women's novel or a 21st century Walden, we do not live in a utopia.

Day 39 / 830 in the evening

I was reminded today of my general unease. When going towards Serpent Mound, we will pass through

Wilmington on our way back. Some days I think, I would like to do so many things but I am cut off from the resources. Other days I think, no, even if given the chance, it would be such a waste to do all that. Like it would be a waste of all those resources. When we go to Serpent Mound, we will walk it in a breeze, it practically won't be enough, will it? We've been working up to moving beyond this kind of easy walk, going around the neighborhood several times a week, going on a new walk each week, with crests and valleys, with creeks and inner woods within woods. The other day when we returned from our daily walk, I got a whiff of myself and was amazed how much cold heat my body generated, how that cold heat generated this supple scent, my evaporated sweat. Did I mark some territory on the way out? Was I self-conscious when the one stared on a little too long at our neighbor's open garage? Why am I afraid of being perceived as an intruder?

I felt exhilarated today when I woke up and received responses, actual responses, one of which I was surprised to come in at all, let alone so quickly. When I say exhilarated, I mean it made my whole body tingle and my heart beat faster. Like I haven't felt that way in a long time. Before going to bed, I finally decided to send my message out into the blue. But it wasn't out of the blue that I felt the urge to. The truth is, I had drafted up a version of the message almost a week ago but never sent it out, and wasn't sure if I ever would. I shared it with one other person, not because I wanted feedback on whether or not I should send the message out, but because it was an addendum to an existing memo that I've been working on. Mostly I thought it would help provide a little padding for exactly what the phases of the project might include. The truth is, even before I drafted up the message almost a week ago, I had this idea in the back of my mind that I could have this project, not the project I've come to think of today as the project, not that, but now, even as I say that, I guess the project I had in the back of my mind for the past year also belongs to the project I've come to think of today as the project. About a year ago, what I thought of as a potential project then never came to fruition, I guess in part because it didn't have this larger project to enfold it. Not that every project has to be constellated into another larger project, but in this case, it just makes sense. The mechanics of it weren't in order, I just jumped right in and started reaching out to people individually, and then I never followed up. This time around, I hesitated, I didn't know if it would ever happen, I had forgotten actually about all those individual messages I sent, I didn't see the connection, for a minute I convinced myself it could be something that never happens, that is, just an idea.

But then last night, I was nearing the end of a chore, a chore that has become really mixed up with rest for me, and anyway I felt the urge to put down the chore and return to the draft of the message from last week. I still hesitated, but then it was ready and I felt ready and I felt I needed to do this and this was actually what had been missing or something and so it was sent. Then it was another night of taking a while to fall asleep. Sometimes you will stay in bed and your mind is cluttered and the cluttering actually makes it impossible to stay awake so the system takes over to wash you away. Sometimes there is enough clarity amidst the remaining clutter that it promises a solution so it's almost irresponsible or wasteful to not stay up and give that solution the opportunity of being found. It almost never happens that you reach it, but I guess that's the sleeper's conundrum. That's when my days are longest but not always most full.

The promise towards a solution of last night was actually a great example or reminder of why it's important to take this new way of living seriously. And by seriously I mean think through the different exclusions that occur with this new way of living, the exclusions and pitfalls and hypocrisies. In committing to this new way of living, can we aim towards a macrocosmic solution still and if we can aim towards a macrocosmic solution does t mean this new way of living hasn't been truly committed to? Does it mean we haven't properly defined what this new way of living must exclude? In committing to this new way of living, is the purpose to aim towards a microcosm? I could see my life flying away in either case. I could see my life flying past me whether I committed to this new way of living microcosmically or whether I committed to this new way of living and endeavored to partner up with someone on devising a macrocosmic solution to the same problems that our new way of living are also somehow rooted in.

What's ever troubling is the fact that I know deep down the macrocosmic solution would solve some of our personal problems, it would mean we wouldn't fight over a bottle of water, it would mean we wouldn't fight over lightbulbs, and I could contribute to the macrocosmic solution but then I would no longer be committing to this new way of living. I mean really committing.

If and when we hear the news that it's over, and we will, I won't celebrate. That was my premonition. In every case that can be marked by probability, sure, I would have envisioned myself celebrating, I have written out my dreams. But now that we have fought one last time, I won't celebrate when it's over and we're finally past the gate.

Day 44 / 2 in the morning

At first the bathroom door was open and the bath was running and I was ok with it because that's kind of nice you know to hear the bath running and to know someone is making use of it and to be near and all but then the philosophers started talking out of the radio and then it was not so nice but I did give it a chance anyway because it was kind of enticing anyway. Like I was still able to do my chores. But it's one of those things where gradually I was unable to do them more and more. And so I became resentful quite quickly. Like quickly I realized how late it was and how unfocused I had become. The unfocused state had really started earlier but it didn't help hearing the philosophers talking. It wasn't even what they were talking about that was spectacularly enticing but how they were talking about it and it wasn't even how they were talking about it that was spectacularly enticing so the fact that I found it enticing was really a puzzle. Maybe the puzzle bothered me. Anyway I went to close the door, or I asked if I could close the door or if it would be too dark, and then I just tried it when I didn't get any response. It was better already, I could feel the promise of less distraction. But of course it was too dark so I had to open the door.

Lately I have been craving a smoke again. Not even the inhale of it because it was the inhale of it that first turned me away. Staying up at night thinking what my lungs were turning into. Don't look up the photos. I would look at the photos and then try to close my head and then I would stay up turning in circles until I thought I could feel the smoke eating away at me from my lung to my brains, everything. It's been many revolutions since I've had a smoke and usually I don't crave it at all, except every now and then, and that's how I know I'm in a kind of mood. The mood of smoking and having flavored pancakes right out of your hands and the dried syrup on top. It's my version of soft cheese and jam. I could never eat soft cheese and jam without destroying my health. I don't know how anyone could. Everyone says it's all in the drink but I always had a drink and I know for certain that didn't help.

In the community, I imagine there will be a special kind of cheese in the fridge too. Not at all times of course, though I would like there to be, but whenever it should be available. Perhaps the point of the community is for us to always be able to have cheese in the fridge without destroying our health. Friends will join us, other members of the community, for nightly meals, they will bring dessert instead of cigarettes, or other conveniences from the city perhaps, or maybe they will bring us cheese, who knows. Clothes, dresses even. We will have to decide whether we will allow our friends to smoke at the table, it shouldn't be a problem for most of them now that they are all thinking of their health as well. I wish nothing but the best for them but sometimes I wish I could be a little voyeur in my own house, remember the good old days.

There is another kind of community that is very quick at talking, whether around the table or around a hole in the ground, almost too quick. You get a sense that their jokes go very far back but also that they are completely fresh, possibly even made up on the spot. How do they do it? Smoke and not dream of smoke? This community isn't trying to leave anyone out, on the contrary, you might see new members at any given gathering. It's funny because on one hand our community is not modeled off of this community at all but on the other hand there are certain aspects honored in this community that I wouldn't mind on occasion bringing into ours. I say this but instantly I know I can't describe what that aspect might be. Certainly not a respect for the lateness of the night.

Today I began planning what to bring with me when we begin our new life. Technically it won't begin exactly this fall but this fall will be a foray into it. As I begin to think of what I will bring I begin to image the space of the fall more and as I begin to image the space of the fall more I begin to smile, a smile came to me. I begin to plot out exactly how the week would go. What we would eat, what food we would buy ahead of time, what I could keep stocked, what I could bring to stock the new place, how to make it cozy, how possible it would be to make it cozy, and then I begin to think of the configuration of all the different places within the community. And it makes me smile. And I have planned out a timeline for the entire week... When we could leave, when we could arrive, when I could run over to drop things off, to get the key, when I could be done setting everything up, when I could go pick up food for the week, when I could arrive back at our new spot after getting food for the week, when we could venture into our new town to get a sense of it and amble around. Though it will be a new adventure for us, we are going there to work, and the community has a hold everywhere we'll go.

Most of the things I will be bringing with me to make our setup cozy I already own but there are a few items on my list I need to procure. It's funny, kind of like how the philosophers were actually discussing this... There are certain things you start thinking about procuring because it makes you feel cozy but then at a certain point the coziness becomes unnecessary because it's really a distraction from the real purpose of the community. Yes, there is something important about the coziness of the community, but at a certain point the coziness becomes a trap. And I noticed myself going into that zone today, at first I was aware of the need for caution, but then almost immediately I fell for the secuction, it wasn't even much of an obstacle getting there. Somehow I am aware of the seduction yet maybe I think I can do it in a way that maintains the connection with the community, that isn't doing it to prove myself to the community, to seduce the community. But come on… isn't there always an element of that?

And isn't there also an element of what we think we deserve? Of how we want to go out? There's a lot of debate now about things like the word deserve in the community. I think it's an important debate. For example, can we deserve a bad thing? Sure. There are members of the community whose hands I don't even know what they look like and yet here I am imagining how the coziness of this space will seduce them. For example. What am I pretending I don't want to get out of this? How much are we willing to spend? Would we set a budget?

I have enlisted the help of people who have been around in the community longer than I have, some of them already departed, some of them still active members, some of them passive members, some of them active-passive. If you are part of the community

then this makes sense to you I am reminded. So I
have enlisted their help to make difficult decisions
concerning which configurations of space will ulti-
mately make me a more active participant in the
community and which will make me more passive. I do
not tell them whether I want to be active or passive,
I believe some assume it is the former, I believe
some assume it is the latter, or perhaps they do not
assume but project their own wishes onto me and
bypass assumption altogether. Mostly I am concerned
about temperature, proximity to different groups of
community members, lighting, and privacy. How could
it be another way?

Day 66 / 1030 at night

It's become one of those days that I fear the most.
It's been so long since I haven't been so habituated
to walking down to the mailbox every hour. I do it now
without even thinking, the way I used to grab a ciga-
rette. And it's been several weeks since I've missed
a cigarette. Before that it was several revolutions.
What do I hope for when I go down to the mailbox?
To find a kitten there? No. I don't know what I would
do if I was faced with that. Cry or scream it isn't
clear. Bring back a plate of milk maybe if there were

any left. I'd like to think I would do such a thing... Even if the good news came, what would it take for the good news to be good enough to change anything? My hopes are dwindling and I have to tell myself, you are lucky. My hopes are dwincling and I have to say to myself, continue. When really I notice I don't even need to say anything to myself anymore. I go down to the mailbox, I find there are only coupons or letters from the department of sanitation, which go days without being touched or opened, because all of their threats are empty, there is nothing they can do, or I get a notification of bad news, and then I carry on with myself. I carry myself on. Yes, every now and then, if it is really bad, it affects me, sure. But what qualifies as really bad? It would be really bad I guess if it's coming when I least expect it. Like I was just content somehow that morning and I could have even been singing a hymn on my way down to the mailbox. It would have to be really bad, like something that is already dwindling. Like I am running out of bullets. How do I keep carrying on? I guess by knowing deep down I have no other choice, and by planning for this major change in our lives.

Today I had intended to think more about this major change but I couldn't bring myself to really think through it. Every time I tried to, I just wanted to make more little changes to the plans instead, I didn't want to think, I wanted to just make decisions instead, look at little trinkets, look at things that don't really affect this major change at all, but at the same time seemed somehow like they were the only things I had to do. I don't feel bad about it. And what's funny is that later in the day, during our checkin, when asked to talk about the patterns I see, I couldn't say anything. Nothing could come out though I tried in earnest. Me, the one who usually carries on and on about the patterns, when asked about them, I couldn't tell her about one. Not one.

I know that any day now there will be a load of news for us, and experience tells me not to expect the odds to weigh in our favor. Anyway this is not an area where odds really matter. That is to say, odds are useless generally when the numbers are what they are in this case. But we have never paid much mind to statistics, for if we did we would have never gotten to where we are. We have inherited statistics, too. But that's the funny thing. This feeling this week of thinking, oh, look where we've gotten. Look how far we've gotten. And yet this feeling that I don't feel any different actually. Or maybe I felt a little different at first but quickly that feeling completely wore off in due. The people around me. They have no idea what I'm talking about. If I told them this just now, they would roll their eyes or say, get away. Or be nice but feel themselves itching beside me. (/) I know how that feels.

Maybe in the first day or two I had a certain sense of oh(,/...) I'm floating.(..) Or... oh... I could be floating... So I stepped away from it a bit(,/...) let myself step away from all of it and take a look around. And I did. I took an inventory, looked through all my belongings, or what I thought or think of as my belongings, and it was like that gave me space to see what I would like to belong to, what I would like to belong to me. But I didn't stop to think, no... that cannot ever belong to me, that... that I can never belong to. (")Look what I've done.(") Or something...

And I have been warned. I've been warned already. I didn't want to just float along, not on this sense or feeling of oh I'm floating. Not that I ever did that ever. But I kind of did. And... sometimes... you don't have a choice and, sometimes, you do have a choice and sometimes I've floated along because I didn't have a choice and sometimes I floated along because I had a choice but maybe I wasn't thinking. But now I've been warned. So what scares me is floating along on this feeling of floating. What scares me is what's next, what's not next. What scares me is how far away everything is, not how close, because it's both. It's both close by and far away, I know. And I know better than to expect anything to really change beyond this imaginary demarcation. What's not imaginary, though, is right now. What's not imaginary is what I am thinking right now, not even what I am doing. Though it's not really true because what I am doing is thinking.

I wanted to write her a thank you note. Maybe I still have time. I have played it out in my head already how this might happen. I have played out in my head how meeting each other on this totally unrelated occasion also might happen. Maybe she will be disappointed or frustrated of who I am after we meet. I can think all of these things, but when the time comes, I can never say them. Not the disappointment or frustration, the background's background. Is it that it wouldn't make sense in any other dimension that makes it extraordinary now? The fact that it can make no sense at all, come across as totally wrong, and yet right now it can make complete sense, and come across as totally decent, that makes it so extraordinary? This is at least my hunch.

I see the people I see and I cannot make an excuse to say that the life we are planning is taking me away from them. It is my choice. I cannot make any excuse and say the life we are planning makes it so that I cannot have time to be accountable to them. I thought I caught something today about anger and forgiveness and it isn't completely applicable to this but I want to say something about anger and forgiveness and friendship and now... Is everyone a piece of work like this?

Sometimes I start to get worried when I hear something and I take this something as a sign for bad news. Today I read something about clairvoyance and I thought why yes I can get behind that, there are clairvoyants in my family, of course. It is unclear, however, whether this skipped a generation or not. In the past, I have sat here with an enigmatic feeling, a feeling of longing, a feeling of desperation perhaps, and I have made grand plans based on this desperation, and then I have stepped back and said, be logical, be practical, and then I have stepped forward and said, I am logical, I am practical, and then continued to believe I could manifest a longing into reality. I could manifest what was longed for of belonging to belong. How many times did that happen? Almost never. Never. This time, the feeling was in the background, this time, it was in the background in that it was nowhere near as strong, or maybe it was but I was too busy planning for other things, I was busy, so I didn't have time to step backwards and forwards and to doubt and to be encouraged and to be eaten up by longing and to be allayed by encouragements of manifestation. If I stop worrying, will it go away? If I stop worrying, will the sign I fear to be a bad sign become a good sign?

Day 70 / unmarked

I'd like to say come on we've all teared up imagining not us saying goodbye to life but those we imagine loving us as they say goodbye to the dead version of us, tearing up as they do so too, either upon hearing the news of our death and opting to send flowers, or less likely, in actually attending our funeral in person. Would this be forbidden in the dead version? I know most people are better than me in this way. I'm sure there is something to unravel here but it's above my pay grade and the unraveling I think is the cheaper shot. I've heard a lot of talk about unraveling and at times it has even appealed to me.

I think of her now, her, the one who, for the greater part of the movement, had probably not had death on her mind at all until she did, until everyone around her did, and then death was not a cloudy thing, it was not something to just have on one's mind, it was something to prevent taking your baby away. For many years, when I was going somewhere, like perhaps taking a long ride, or especially when taking a short ride, for short rides are frequently made by smaller and therefore more vulnerable entities, entities more vulnerable to the elements for example, anyway when I would do this, I would mail out a scribbled will to someone I trusted most. As though I had anything to leave behind. It was very important to me however that what little I had was left in the right hands. Lately this has not been something I've done so much, even though I have stronger feelings about dying unexpectedly now than I did when I was younger, and the feelings veer in the direction of being not too thrilled about it. And yet my body has finally arrived because I could be dying soon. And yet I can't imagine her having this love affair but maybe we are to fill that in ourselves. I can't imagine her taking off her clothes to capture the last vestiges of youth, perhaps because that belongs to the story behind the story.

When you don't have a lot, you deal with a constancy of worry that you almost take on an air of "it'll work out because we have to make it work, we always get by anyway." When you just have enough, you begin to think, "what if we had more than just enough, what if we had a little more." And when you have enough plus a little extra, you begin to worry about all kinds of things, you begin to think you need all kinds of things, a different type of pillow, a different type of shoe, a different type of water bottle. I learned a new word this week but I forgot to practice it. One is making fun of me again.

I've noticed that people who are good people, good inside, but maybe a little lost or in too deep have started looking at me for the wrong things. They hear something from me and they expect to look at me for something that inevitably won't be there. I don't know what to say to these people. Do they feel sorry for me or have I confused them or made them think twice? Are they thinking what I'm thinking? It's hard to explain too the ways that I have compromised at every turn of the road. Literally, through the leaps, it seems almost futile to try to explain the ridiculous ways that I have compromised, the details.

I was looking at the gills of a mushroom the other day and thinking of all those spores that come from it, with its genetics, and how someone described it to me as winning the lottery, the lifespan of a spore, how much like winning the lottery it is for a single spore to just so happen to be carried into a new environment with the right conditions, the right nutrients, to begin to become something beyond its spore life. I even read that people are often surprised to find that two mushrooms belonging to the same species technically, genetically, can be found in totally different environments in different parts of the world, mutually flourishing, and that scientists still don't know how to explain a lot of these mysteries.

You'd look at a family, for example, and you'd see a family with a mommy and a daddy and three kids, for example, and you couldn't say, look how one of these kids turned out, or look how two of these kids turned out, and why is there one black sheep, and you couldn't say, for example, look, for all of you we did the same thing, didn't we, so why is one of them different, why are one of you different, or, look, look at the other families, no one is perfect, no one has an excuse.

It's hard to tell now whether we are truly living the way we set out to, whether we are living the opposite of the way we set out to but find ways to justify it, find ways to explain it away as the way we always set out to, find ways to say we have no choice or we deserve it or we aren't bad people really, or whether it was always just an idea to guide us, an idea to guide us as we fumbled into the opposite way.

And I start to think what we could be losing is each other. I start to think we don't know a thing about each other, the way we operate on a circadian rhythm, for example. Sometimes you want to be reminded where someone comes from to justify their perspective or even their perspective on other perspectives. At first when you heard the words "correct perspective" you felt disappointment, maybe even a tinge of anger, and soon after, it became a sad feeling, a sad feeling for someone. You were reminded then of the room with four human bodies cramped together, you were reminded of a room for the mommy the daddy the son and the daughter, and you were reminded of three families with the mommy the daddy the son and the daughter squeezed into a building with three rooms for each family, a shared kitchen, a shared bathroom and you were reminded of ten years where all this squeezing occurred. No one even comes close, no one even comes as close. And yet we're all squeezed together. We're all desperate but some of are more willing. Oh yeah...

We went off course but then I was brought back to my original point. We walked by the carousel under the bridge but then we returned and stopped in front of the carousel. We stopped when we heard a train passing over us over the bridge and then when it had passed over we all laughed, taking someone's cue, and then we proceeded. We went ahead of everyone else and then the rest followed us a few blocks away. I realize I never asked myself, where are they now? I realize now I never needed to know where exactly are they? If I stop to ask myself now, I would have to guess that it would have been a city, but a mid-sized city, a city that was big enough to not feel like a town, but a city that was small enough where two people could meet in a way that you could follow from beginning to end.

(/ₚ) (.) (,)

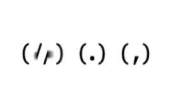

Day 244 / 2 in the afternoon

We are here now. Not where we said we would be. But also not where we never thought of. We are here. It is still unknown whether we will be on our way. Whether we will be tortured. But for now we are in a stand still. There are no more packages. When I need main street, I go there instead. Because we are completely deserted. And they rely on us taking care of each other. It has been established. We've begun to see that. They cannot continue without this reliance on our willingness to do whatever it takes for each other. They cannot continue as an entity that survives by way of offsetting without our willingness to offset what allows them to be an untouchable entity. So at what point do we say, enough is enough, pass on, let each other down in order to not allow the entity to keep working.

This morning, our plan was to go to main street, one of them, to sit down, be away from each other while also being right beside each other, and then check in. But it didn't work out. We would interface intermittently with each other over the course of deciding the procedure of going to main street, going to a body of water, going to procure food and other essential items, but we would never even get that far. Somehow, soon enough, it would become about where we came from, too, except this time, it would be relevant. Despite claims on the contrary, it would make sense to bring up where we came from in relation to what we were doing to and for each other now. Now we are still in the intermittent place. As we were finally on our way out, as we had finally met some kind of point of diffusion, as we had finally decided there would be no main street today, only passing through main street, if need be, only passing through main street if it was necessary to pass through it in order to get through at all to a body of water, something changed. We realized one of us was wearing the wrong thing. We realized we forgot to bring some crucial items. All of this would both add to the diffusion as it would add to the aggregate yet delayed resentment. By the time we had settled on a route, one of us had already begun aggressively cleaning as one of us had begun noticing the issue of near future caloric intake. I could have been done now. Everything that needed to be done in order for us to move on could have been done, in one way, but now time is diffused. We could make it a good thing now...

We were heading towards what I had believed to be one of the main streets and then we came to what looked completely abandoned. So it was an abandoned section that could merely be disjointed and not too far away from the main street, disjointed but connected underneath. We found out later anyway that it was just that. I said, we could be the next neighbors to join this community, to make something of meaning here, of sustenance. What would we even make? It could just be an homage to us... It was like this conversation diffused our anger, our hands touched, and we were a unit again.

Then we began to route ourselves towards a place that is becoming more and more familiar to us even if it has not become a part of our memory yet. We needed some help getting there. Turn right, turn left, turn right, stay on the road. I can't remember where the conversation went after that. It didn't matter. We missed a turn but then we went back and soon arrived. Already we had a better sense of the place, we were already less tentative, we already felt we needed less permission to set ourselves down somewhere, that we were not intruders, that any contact we made with others there would not intrude upon them or us. We found a place between two spheres. We sat on the edge that could have connected them. We began to settle in. Another arrival eased us.

Said hello. Not to us but to another group. This eased us already.

So many unknown creatures here—have they always belonged here? As long as we have? How long does it take for pollination to occur? I am noticing the sounds of pollination and how easily these sounds can be confused for other more menacing sounds and how other sounds we have thought of as menacing really would only be so under a particular set of circumstances. Apparently everyone is afraid of that. We have been here for what seems like less than one hour and everyone has almost been kind. We are surrounded by kindness and we are surrounded by judgment but judgment can also be the purest form of kindness, true judgment.

It is hard to tell whether we are the loudest things here or whether what we fear is an intrusion has already been anticipated or adapted to beyond our self-consciousness. Nothing that has touched me here has hurt me. I have asked the one if the one is going to be ok. I don't know is the answer. It is jarring at first to be in this place and then soon we realize we have to adjust our idea of peace and control. Just now we saw what appeared to be a miraculous act of navigation on the most local of levels. And then we realized it was actually a public display of affection. What appeared to be a solitary act became or was made apparent to us as doubles. But they were not equals. What we thought was a single existence became a question of whether one can coexist within oneself. Have we received our weekly vitamin d? Have we ever? I am neither not ready to leave nor am I ready to go.

We get the feeling through intuition and words we've heard that some of the friendlies here could be coming from the same place as us. Through various things picked up we believe this is a temporary excursion for them, a day of rest. Is this our day of rest too? How? We find the most rest while working through rest, resting through work. One of us does. But the one's working community has sung and sung and made banners and made anthems to commemorate or remind the community of the community's contributions back to other communities who have been singing for a long time, singing without banners, without anthems, without even listeners the one's working community has utilized these contributions as a way to lure and to set itself aside from other communities. But if anyone stops marching, the community ceases.

This shuffling back and forth, this shuffling that requires so many past lives, so much sustenance, so much vitamin d. Like we have misunderstood ourselves. Like we have sat, heavy, with idle, and thought. We have procured enough materials now. We can get there again. Tomorrow we will procure again.

I have not gone to the supply shop yet. I have gone to the nursery and to the army discount store. But I have not gone to the various supplies shops yet. I have set the plants out outside, or, rather, one of them set out the plants in front of the building for me. One fern, two palms, and yarrow. She has a relationship with yarrow, a personal relationship. Still I don't know if I'll ever make it there and a part of me worries I will have disappointed them, I will have made them feel like their time was wasted with me, like I was just wasting their time. I would be an idle person, so idle…

The more I think about the main event the more I think what we are celebrating is not a beginning but an ending. The more I think about the main event the more I think what we are celebrating is not a beginning or an ending, not for us, but an ending for those we have known and held onto and whom we have needed in order to know, an ending between us and those we have come to know just each other through. To be given a chance. What do we owe them? Everything? Is it wrong that they have no idea this is more of an ending than it is a beginning? Who are we beholden to here? Who are we cuckolding?

Sometimes I think we've gone back and forth so much between leaving a place temporarily and leaving a place permanently that we've forgotten soon we won't have a choice, or the choice will be made for us anyway, or we will indeed make a choice but it won't even seem like we're making a choice anymore. Sometimes I think we already made a choice by not making a choice and so now what we thought was the worst possible circumstance is now no longer so foreboding, is now something that we can put up with, if necessary, before we get to where we will wind up eventually, not to where we go. Somehow the foreboding is no longer something that weighs daily on us, though we are aware of its shape, though we are aware of template, somehow we have become too busy with the daily task of going back and forth, of keeping up with the needs of the temporary encampment and with maximizing our meaning here, which sometimes conflict with the needs of a less temporary future encampment. This is a place that could become familiar to us if we dared. This is a place that could also become forced upon us. That's all.

There is a restaurant on main street I am taking cues from, there is a restaurant on the main street towards main street that I am learning from. Could I go in and ask if there is a place for me there? Where would I begin? It's not that I would cease to pursue this other main line, this main line I have had to set stones down for, but it is possible, I think, to pursue two main lines simultaneously, and to the end. And is it fair if one of them becomes a backup plan? It is best to become mesmerized so that you become confused as to whether or not the backup plan was ever really a backup plan, or an exit strategy.

Sometimes I think our neighbors don't really see us as neighbors at all because they figure we won't be staying past the season, not because they know us, not because they know anything about our exit strategy, but because people who stay in this house are frequently passing through, so they're just used to seeing people come and go frequently. It's not their fault. It should also be noted that we did not take the initiative to go over there when we first arrived to introduce ourselves. How many of us can fit behind the wall that separates us from them? The grass is allowed to grow up to the knees here and the mulberry tree is open to the entire street for picking. I find it most fun to get a ladder and go one by one. I say this but I'll never do it. I am a perfect voyeur instead.

Why doesn't the neighbor approach me? Maybe I have never looked troubled enough as I stand by the mailbox? One has been approached several times now, one has heard many of the neighbor's stories, one has heard some of the neighbor's stories about the other neighbors, like the neighbors who are always fighting, and one has heard some of the neighbor's stories about the neighbor's memories of camping. We wonder what the neighbor's role is here, is the neighbor in charge of things or does the neighbor work for other people here who are in charge of things? We have our suspicions. There is something about the neighbor that inspires a mouthful of mulberries. There is something about the neighbor that inspires a sorrowful feeling and shirt open, guts hanging out. How can we derive what we derive from the neighbor's neighbors without knowing exactly their relations to each other, though we have our suspicions, how can we stand here, apart, behind, away, go past, give each other looks, as though, always as though... while also knowing the same reason we have a haven at all right now is related to the reason why the streets are so broken here, is related to the reason why the music is played loudly with disregard, is related to the reason why there is someone outside fixing their vehicle, having lemonade.

I could continue, to live off the good grace of others, off of what has gotten me far enough to live off the good grace of others. Is that what the training was for? I could be a permanent guest in other words but then I would only be offsetting my own needs, whose other needs, for example, would I even be capable of offsetting as a permanent guest? Would I be able to offset another's offspring? On the other hand, we have sometimes even beguiled ourselves with the possibility of using the exigencies of guests instead. In this scenario, the guests would be paying for us to live where we already and almost live. Having guests or a consistent flow of guests would give us a reason and the means to live somewhere ourselves. So what is offset would simply be able to belong to us.

It was never explicitly stated, no, that we would be officially in charge of looking after this house. But it is implied nonetheless. It is implied that we would only be fucking ourselves over if we chose to let everything go. Our exigencies made it so that in about a month we would be checked in on and depending on what was found out of us, of what we did with our time here, it would play a part in our ability to move on, whereas our host has put herself in a very good position. It's like we have been cuckolded but there is no point in making a fuss of it. Besides, we are leaving soon and it doesn't make sense to try to find another place to go. Even if we have been cuckolded. It's nice to have the place to ourselves. To have a place to clean aggressively. In part for ourselves right now, in part for ourselves in the near future.

If I chose to just allow my weariness to be a reason to allow, to make allowances on one defining thing that does not define me, on one show-stopping piece that does not show who I am, I will have shown what I am willing to allow, shown my place in the world to allow, to not allow, and that's maybe all.

Yesterday we were right beside each other and it was late but our timelines were somehow mostly in sync even though we were on totally different levels or maybe for the first time we were actually as close as we would ever get in terms of levels. Or maybe we were just both content in the cruelty of the world that we can't control. Anyway, the one began reading aloud to me. I didn't want it at first, and I still didn't want it fully when I said ok, but then, once it began, I was with it. It made complete sense to me. What, in another world, in another world prior to the exigencies of thinking of this new way of living, for example, would have been felt to me as a waste of time, a draining of my time that otherwise could be used somehow more productively, became exactly the work. Anyway, even there, in that reading aloud, in that space of eclipsing, I heard the word... Miracle... Oh no...

I have just now started making a plan to smuggle some of our sustenance out to the other encampment. I don't want to be unfaithful but I have been keeping tabs and it has become indisputable that certain items are spoiling when they could have been shared with the other encampment. If I didn't think

there were sure to be extras, I wouldn't offer from
our pile. If I didn't think there were sure to be stuff
leftover for the birds, I wouldn't sneak around.

Today about an hour or two before our checkin time,
as scheduled, one and I began the exercise that
needed to be complete before our checkin time today.
Apparently we had different ideas of what would count
as fulfilling the exercise, apparently we had differ-
ent ideas of what the purpose of the exercise was at
all. In truth, both of us were a bit lost. For me, on
my end, it was a test of patience, a way to check my
anger. I think that for the one it was a way to test
one's sense of distrust, a way to let go the need to
do everything according to the right way. What is the
right way? What is the right way to do this exercise?
the one kept asking, wanting to stop. But I wanted
to figure out as we went. The truth is, neither of us
had "fun." So we missed the point. Or we missed part
of the point, since a part of the point was also the
exercise of it, but the point we missed was that it
was a chance for us to have fun. I guess we forgot
to mention that we haven't been doing much of that
lately. Even our time of leisure is timed these days.

Yesterday, for example, we actually talked about what
would happen if we actually had a baby and that baby
lived and if we died while that baby lived then who
would be the next of kin to take on the responsibility

of making sure that baby would continue to live. We actually talked about that, like it was no big deal, as we were walking away from a place of serenity and things that we could only describe as dragonflies, because I guess we had gotten our fill. Was this just idle talk? Or were we making a game plan somehow?

The point is that even in this moment of leisure there was little feeling of fun. I mean, after all, what counts? I am realizing now that, in a way, our aimlessness still requires the layout of an aim. Whether we are together, by ourselves, or with other members of the community, whether we are together and I am with the one, or I have left the one by oneself and they feel totally cut off from the community. As though I am the only link to it. And yet it really isn't fair to compare our aimlessness to the aimlessness of the community. Otherwise, there wouldn't be such a cloak and there wouldn't be so many swords showing up just when I am smiling.

I don't think anyone in the community would admit beyond a sphere of two, at most three, if that's where it has to go, if that's where the mood must have it, that the question of reputation is so deeply ingrained in the community, the question of reputation is so deeply linked to the question of attention and yes that word generosity. But I have felt it undeniably. As in, I have felt this change of attention, this coming around to attending to a person, after that attention has been considered earned. I guess it's hard to get away from that but I would hope that this sense of how attention might be earned would reside more in the question of honesty, not just reputation. Like, the more you surround yourself with the same type as yourself, the more your sense of kindness actually just becomes a sense of being nice, not kind at all, not honest. Otherwise, why are we even here? What did we think we could get out of this community? Confirmation?

Besides, some people have no idea how far the community has come. Even if it is still very far from being any sort of utopia. But, nonetheless, some people seem to believe the gesture for celebration is enough, is a reason to celebrate in and of itself, a reason for us to follow through all the way, some people seem to believe there is a way to separate the celebration from the story, or that what links them is a gesture, and that's all. They don't see the fault in that. There is a fissure in the community today. Not that there was never a fissure before. But today the fissure is called one thing by community members who speak on behalf of the entire community when the members who are not speaking feel the fissure should not be called this one thing, it should not be called one thing at all. But now is not my time to enter.(..)

I was trying to think what of the one is so divisive. One is pure. One, in the beginning, never screamed. In the beginning, when I screamed, the one would question their faith. And so one was pure. And yet one remains pure, too. We share a piece of the jade. Sometimes, this piece of jade could be the jade that prevents us from entering the community, or it could be the jade that at first lets us in by some virtue, that actually lets us in wholly by virtue, and then, eventually, ostracizes us. Or… it could be the jade that allows us in by way of some vested authority yet nobody really trusts us for a really long time despite this investiture, no one trusts until they realize it actually all makes sense, that actually the purity makes sense, why the piece of jade totally makes sense on us.

Because the one and I aren't often on the exact same page about the piece of jade, not because we purposefully don't want to be, but because our communities require us to sometimes see one side of it only, require us to sometimes rest it on one side more purposefully, as though for protection, sometimes it almost seems like what separates us from each other also keeps us linked. We are each other's access points to our own strangleholds. Maybe because what separates us from each other separates us from our separate communities more, maybe because what makes us rest in each other has turned

my scream into a song, even if often we're confused
by this theory of separation, confused and wonder
how much of it is just our own mental state, our own
self-consciousness. That's a song too though.

Everyone wanted to talk about the setup of the
spheres and monitors. I must admit I did not pay
much attention to two of the monitors. I could only
pay attention to the fighting of voices and the way
that it was difficult to tell whether they were fighting at all or whether they were just trying to find a
way to coexist. There is a difference. Even if the one
doesn't believe this. There is. I wrote down a little
note and passed it on. I rewrote the sloppy part.
To be honest, it wasn't until after the fact that I
started to realize what to me felt extraneous.

I had been developing a friendship lately, a friendship with a being that wore their mistakes like a
specialized belt. A living work of art. I think we both
came in with magnets on us, magnets that promised
to move toward each other, but then began to repel.
I don't know what happened. Maybe I have encroached
too much on their other territories or maybe somehow
I just started to come across as rejecting their
offerings. Or maybe the way I communicated to them
was not believable. Remember the piece of jade? I am
trying to describe what it's like to knead something
hard inside of you, knead something like a stone,

without the chance of it ever actually disappearing, without it ever becoming leavened or something, to eat, to react to, like dough, like a doughnut. I almost don't want to try to save it anymore.

If I left now, would I be left with a longing? Each day is new. If I left now, would I be caught? I don't want to live a double life. And I don't think I have to. Why are we given a choice?

It has become increasingly difficult to keep in touch with the ones we had to leave behind. Because I am trying to learn and absorb all I can—without putting up a front either, even if that feels impossible. But I have learned it is better to offer what you have, without holding back, because going in with this you will inevitably hold back anyway and by doing so maybe you can be forgiven for what little or however irrelevant it is you have to offer.

Are we expected to just stand across from someone after they have spoken to a smaller unit of the small community within the larger unit of the large community, say hi, and not expect this encounter to be suggestive? I cannot account for quite a many gestures but if one thing is certain it's that a further list of ingredients will be sure to complicate the scenario, and by complicate, I mean risk losing a focused attention on two entities and their floating relation. Maybe a part of me knew no one would pay attention to these particular entities and their floating relation, or maybe it was just what was within my wheelhouse.

When you go into a new community, is it innocence to expect that community to meet you more than halfway, is it innocence to expect that community to go twice as far as it's already gone in two revolutions? When you go into a new community, is it innocence to expect to tear down that community, that community that has already been torn down, and not for the sake of repair, for the sake of exposure, is it innocence to expect to tear it down and to place your imprint on that community upon entrance? Does innocence descend? Does innocence ask for something without grounds to ask for it? One never warned me but one said something like it was a warning too late.

Some things in this new way of living required saying goodbye to the old way of doing, some aspects of this new way of living still require understanding what was necessary to say goodbye to, understanding what work has already been done, how far we have come, understanding what work was not, what length was not, a gesture, like banter.

What got into me last night? Maybe I am starting to be more honest. With myself, above all. Maybe I am starting to get in touch with a part of myself I would have never before last night, before right now, admitted to being disconnected from. What is it about this new way of living that at first took me away, took me away from myself, and then after a time, brought me back? I don't know, I waver... Sometimes, I think, from a distance, I could lose all of my fear, all of my shyness, and I've seen myself do it, I've seen myself later and I... well, I cringe, but when I forget that it's happened, I dream, I see it, and I think it's so easy, it comes easy to me actually, sometimes now and then I'm ok and it just happens and the two of us aren't even catching up, we are sitting together at the center of a circle, our conversation is a part of the larger conversation and it's also containing its own, I don't know, like gravity...

I tried to explain at some point during our checkin that the friendships, which somehow take me away from my habits, while also bringing out the deepest ones, while also bringing out the best and worst ones, are so important because they make it possible for me to be gotten into. Like, they get into me, I guess, and so even when I say goodbye, I have them in me, somewhere in me, and beyond my recognition sometimes, I start changing. At first, I may seem distant. And then, I come closer. There is friction. And I want more friction. Friction for friction's sake almost. Honestly, it doesn't even have to get me anywhere, it's just the contact that reminds me. I couldn't sleep last night, my eyes were heavy, but my mind kept turning…

I want to make myself available, to offer myself up to run errands, necessary errands, to be a community member who contributes to things that aren't necessarily essential, like soap or food. But here essential also requires a revisiting. Will flowers hereafter be considered essential? Will banners? Just now I realized maybe I have been pushing myself to make a decision on this matter of essential versus not essential. The one just had to add that either way I am selfish, even if it may seem like my desire to do something essential for the community is for the community, it is actually just for myself, it is actually just so I won't feel guilty otherwise.

Why should I be so startled to hear that I am not the only one who has fallen under the weather? I am not the only one for whom being under the weather just seemed like the initial discovery of life, and then it became the backdrop and then eventually I just started to decorate it, or not and I didn't. When I feel less shy and initiate contact, I have to not take it personally if my contact doesn't pierce through. I don't want to pierce anyone.

I'm like an ogre swatting at flies. I can step out of myself too and see the lack of empathy, the redirection of empathy towards the fly, and then only as a result of this, the re-redirection of the empathy towards the ogre. Is this what we came here for? To make friends? Now I think maybe you can let go... of that grasp a bit.

I've heard footsteps roaming the halls here, at odd hours, at sleeping hours, I don't know if someone is just wandering around, trying to find something, anything, or if it's maintenance. Why do I distrust what I also am? Because I have been run through? Was the smile an offering or just something done out of habit, something you couldn't fight, had no reason to? I don't want to be brave. I will fight. I will fight. I want to believe it is someone checking in on me, curious about me, someone who heard I could be staying here, but not the wrong person... Who has access to this building who could even be the right one? I'll never find out, will I?

They have told us this is what the sun will do to you, stay inside. But we have no choice, we have to go out in order to fulfill our duties. There is paperwork, there is washing of linens and shirts, there is attending. When I say I want to make the most out of all the work we put into getting our act together, I realize it means I have to go against the recommendations. I have to move around and expose myself. It would be easy to say that I look around and I watch the way everyone sits together, the way everyone stands beside one another, the way everyone walks past each other and either smiles or doesn't smile, it would be easy to say that it seems to be such a mystery to me. Because it is. I guess that would be easy. But would it be easier to say I am part of this constellation as well? That I take as much as I give.

One said one doesn't want to live here, or no, one said one doesn't know if one could stay here indefinitely, because one doesn't like killing things. How do I tell one that it isn't up to one? We must make the decision together. We must also wait. Or we can make the decision and hope to be able to go back on it if we end up having to be displaced again. I don't want one to be worried. One wants me to be worried. I have told one I will come up with a plan, a provisional plan for an idea, a provisional plan for a backup plan. But I am so busy with things, things which are difficult to explain exactly why they are necessary to repair the community, the community I will have to be cut off from, the community which will disown me, the community I will have to find another way into. Am I confusing the repair of the community with another kind of repair? Am I confusing being busy with obligation? It is hard not to be confused about this.

Now I begin to backtrack, and by backtrack I mean doubt, and by doubt I mean wonder, wonder whether what I said was ok. Is saying aloud what takes half an hour to formulate finally ok? Or are we just trying to constellate things that don't really exist ever? Are we trying so deeply? It's kind of like how sometimes I think the footsteps are coming towards me when in actuality they are moving in the opposite direction but I only realize once the footsteps have arrived at their destination. No one is coming towards me. And sometimes I think I am totally by myself when everyone can actually hear me. Such a nuisance! I didn't realize until now how much it meant to me, to be appreciated, to be trusted. Now I worry I have spoilt it all, that, by living by this code too much, this code that may have something to do with not holding back, even if there inevitably is censorship, not holding back in action, even if inevitably there is censorship in what is said. She was always right, naive... This code of offering even if what you have to offer is nothing. But I fear now that it has gone too far. I fear now that I cannot distinguish between an offering that is nothing and an offering that breaks our trust. Maybe I was confused between trust and appreciation, of course they were never the same thing. Our trust was never earned.

I will learn. I promise I'll learn. I was very cognizant today... periphery. Cognizant but accepting of my own self-consciousness and my own resilience I want to say? People are making their rounds. I am making my round somehow as well, pacing back and forth, coming out near the stadium wafting in the air a bit, is it wafting? and then moving on again, coming out, moving on again. Who is gone? It should come as no surprise that this level of thinking arises from articles of intimate clothing dangling on a chair, or not, because was I really thinking of that until now?

Today after leaving the shop I felt very idle. I said as much. Usually I feel I must head straight away somewhere... whether to my allotted resting place in the narrows by the garden or straight back to our shared resting place in the new town, new for us, but old, old with old streets that are in need of repair. But somehow today I was comfortable with this feeling of idleness and I wanted to announce it, just in one on one moments though. I repeated myself. I feel idle. Maybe from there, because they understood what I meant or something when I said that, I felt I could open up. About nudity... water... underwear. So forth. This idleness took me back in a roundabout way to my allotted resting place, and I had company in a new friend. Maybe I never realized until today how fractured we are now, how this fracture has given some breathing room for us to move between the layers, make real friends.

Are we just psyching each other out? I stay in my lane, they stay in their lane, are we just trusting... that we won't... take it over the line? I was wired one way, so I am the software in part, because of know how in part, but of course that's not the deepest nor the most honest aspect of this tetris. Do I trust myself today? I think the answer is yes. But there is something very vile about this forward motion. Do we really trust our training that much? Is it the training or is it our obligation? Of course we are asking too much.

Something that has come up quite a lot these past few days, or maybe just something I've paid more attention to, is the fact that every now and then someone will mutter something like, it's kind of just getting to that time of year, time of place, when your whole body starts getting covered in welts. If you're just having fun, is there even a funnel? If you're just showing us all of the various angles, how are we to know? Sometimes we can think and we can believe, we must, and keep in mind_.

I am immensely conflicted by the information that has been able to be processed so far but I admit much of it remains cloudly. I shouldn't hold myself up to this arbitrary standard, arbitrary expectation. So what if I didn't do x y z and it is such and such day of the week and I have some belief that such and such day of the week holds a particular value, that such and such day of the week carries a particular weight. I can't describe it honestly. It's like describing a lucky number. Why, for example, does 83 mean something to me? It's been that way from the beginning. 3 is half of 8. And this was before I was aware of infinity. That's not who I am.

I can tell myself, you are growing, I can tell myself, you can disregard, I can tell myself, what does this matter, I can tell myself, be reasonable, I can tell myself, it's arbitrary, they want you to feel this way, but I still feel this way.

I am realizing now that too many of us are spread out and I have kept the circle too close at the same time. So this will always work against me. I am realizing now that if I add cheese to the shopping basket at night because I cannot rest because I cannot do anything it is because I am craving cheese, my body has a knowledge I never doubted but easily forget. I want to be better than the part of me that itches. I want to be better than the part of me that cannot stop thinking about the itching. It is a mirage however. Around the circle I learned a new word today. Transcend. It seemed very clear to me what it meant, it seemed very

clear their expectations for me. But I still craved and
I itched. I still would.

Anyway if the circle was only ever so big, I guess
it could be infinite. That's what I'm maybe trying to
get at.

It's been days since we saw the mouse, and you know
what they say, when everything is gone, the mouse
goes too, so we thought with the state of things,
it made sense that the mouse we had even named
and gotten cozy over wasn't encountered for several
weeks. Just now I heard the one groan. I guess the
mouse has returned. Sometimes I can't tell if the
way we admonish is a joke, or even who the joke is
aimed at, or if we really want to be cozy with the
mouse, or if we really want what it would take for
the mouse to vacate the premises. We don't really
need to go there.

At the playground a few weeks ago some of our
neighbors or some people who looked like them were
being derelict under the pavilion structure or what-
ever. One was just trying to find a place to count
but it was all too earnest, who would have believed
that, of course. I don't blame one, I don't blame
the neighbors or lookalikes either. They were just
scared because they were derelict and when they got
around to noticing they assumed the worse. They've

heard the news before. One will not be going back there again. One will have to get membership elsewhere to count elsewhere where it is sanctioned I guess to count and no one will be worried you have bad intentions. What a world..

We want to play our part, we want to show our appreciation for those who don't deserve to not be shown our appreciation, like it does become a kind of obligation, for they are not part of the ickiness of the icky part of the show, they are the part that makes it work, and they are the part that helps to give us worth, and then yes, we remember during the showing and announcing of our appreciation the faux pas. Faux pas. How nimble we never were when we wanted to be. Around that. Faux pas. Who? Faux pas. The point I was trying to make has solidified the inability for the obligation to show appreciation as widely as possible to be as wide as possible and yet it does not take away the necessity to participate. We might disappear, I might disappear, but I still have to participate.

Is there inbreeding in the community nowadays? Is there inbreeding in the community if the community members only breed with each other? Then is there not inbreeding in the community if the community members only breed with each other if the community is founded based on a gathering of people from disparate locations, backgrounds, classes, lineages? At what point does this also become inbreeding? I mean how many generations does it take for this to become itself (, to become) inbreeding?

The juice was bad today. I don't know how that keeps happening. It had only been five days since we got it and once again it went bad. One and I both drank it, we didn't want it to go to waste. I think I'll survive. Ten minutes later one was complaining of stomach-aches but I think it was related to something else one has been eating, related to the counting, that I have not myself been eating. I've had enough experience with supplements, enough experience to know, but I didn't want to caution one too much. Besides, one knew going into it already the basic cautions already. It was just a matter of rationalizing the possible benefits against the cautions for one.

Everything feels too calm. Too calm for all the hyper-activity. I wish we could just be lit from underneath. Did I always crouch? Did I always sneak away? I guess I stayed past my allotted time so the sneaking came up( )on me. People behave here like they're used to this place. Am I used to it? It's become a part of me, but I think I could stay here for a thousand years and it still wouldn't be something I'm used to. How many corners are there in a forked building? I guess you have to add and subtract depending what you include, if you include the outdoor space with the puddles, or if you include the other outdoor space with the lot. I didn't really think about it when I approached the building before but now that I think about it, it means people have gotten work... again. We are in the midst of a celebration but not because of this fact.

Why do I speak differently from person to person? I thought I was honest. Or maybe I'm exactly so honest, person to person. I can't tell? Do I crush? Do I crush it? Or do I just want to make sure what I'm saying gets my point across without giving too much away? At this moment the lighting outside has begun to become faded enough for the lamp I brought to make a difference to really meet its moment. But I think the whole project of lamps is now a bust. It's true I wanted to fabricate something that would make someone, when approaching, possibly ask themselves, is this a lamp?, like they would recognize something in that thing that said, oh, is that a lamp? Made them ask that kind of a question. At least we aren't mean.

We left in such a hurry today I forgot to bring the things that help to tell myself it's time... It's time to put things to rest for example. It's not that it's not my job to coat things in a lining that allows a kind of a pill to be swallowed softly, I would do that for, for example, baby, but I guess that just goes to show there is a difference to me between this approach and the approach I might give to someone who's not baby. I think I've found people here are more accepting than I would have imagined. In a way, I did psyche myself out.

I'd like to use the example that's also really a hypothesis of a potential dream. Like I said, there would be two entities I would say, they force each other into corners occasionally. But generally, they have invented also what it means to be cozy. So in the example, one of them seems to be pouring love into one thing. The other is only capable of making fun of this love thing. And they use something else to make fun of them actually, for example, pointing out that the thing that love is pouring into is not what the lover thinks not what the lover thinks they are pouring this love into. But the lover fights back. This plays out continually and the lover continues to pour their love into this one thing. All the time, this lover also pours love into the loved. It even becomes frustrating sometimes, hence, part of the reason for fights. The believable part, of course, is that the other lover pours all their love into the loved, it's just through this way of poking fun, making fun, and, I guess everyone has their own way of saving themselves. Though sometimes it seems wrong to me.

I guess if you're lucky you don't often have to think of temperature. You're under control. Not thinking of what it would be like, what it would even be like, to not have to think about it, to not have to work your way around it. I was just thinking it might be nice to wake up to the noise of grass getting cut by someone at a reasonable hour but seemingly unreasonable to someone who had a bad night of sleep, was lucky to have somewhere to sleep. I guess I'm wondering who might be roaming around tonight and tomorrow, and if it's worth the trouble of staying around for that information.

In years past, we never had a night like this, we never had so many consecutive days and nights like this, anyone could probably tell you, or upon being asked I am sure someone would say it. At the same time, no one talks about it. Maybe no one has asked?

Is it wrong that I never felt made less special even if their attention turned easily toward anyone? I didn't. I thought, not only does that make sense, not only is that their right, I feel special anyway. Before, when I was technically more diversified, I didn't feel more in control. And, on top of that, I wasn't. I know. I saw it in the way things would happen to my body without my premonition. Which is unacceptable because of all the palmistry that is background in the old community. That old community.

Something one has always pointed out during our stay here, our stay anywhere actually, yes, before and after, is the fact that my camera is often on... I don't use my camera no but it is often on... So what, I say, it was on for another reason I say. But one is concerned. If they want something they can grip, I am starting to understand why I could be that. And why, before, I didn't offer myself up quite so much. My friend, my dear friend, why, she's on one timeline, and sometimes we're on the same timeline, and sometimes we are, but sometimes when it comes down to exact minutes, it makes a major difference, I don't know, it maims, and I have to back out.

I don't really know how to describe it without talking about what happens when people are dancing at the center and when people break off into tiny units beyond the center. Something of course always happens there, whether it's a becoming tired of the dancing, or no longer feeling like you can really dance without overthinking it, or simply feeling the wrong song is playing now, so wrong that you can't stop thinking about how wrong of a song it is to be playing now, so that the thinking does become too much and it is impossible for you to stay in the center without becoming a stone. If I looked at the stone, what would I see?

A friend of mine said something last night about how even when the tiny units break off from the center, it's kind of like they still contain an incredible force, a kind of gravity I guess, and so it's hard to go around from unit to unit. For me, it's exactly that, it's practically not possible at all. I don't know if I just stick or if I am sucked but I would say it sometimes seems I just wrap on like a leech and then I'm sucked too.

It is hard, after going so far in, carrying so much of what to remember, sleeping for many days, drinking water for many days, drinking juice, however spoiled, to assess and to hear and to absorb and to make sure we can go back in without letting that farness dictate our movement from place to place. Sometimes I feel I'm just picking one thing up at a time, picking one thing up, then putting it down, then moving on, picking up another thing. Other times I see how I pick one thing up, set down a part of it even if it seems like I have set down all of it, carry it on with me, carry that part that was not set down, and then I pick up another thing again. And around around I go... It is funny... that... I never got dizzy this way... Maybe that's what would keep me from getting dizzy?

All the while, how do I manage this trickery, this trade, and still make sure we are conducting ourselves according to each other? Or that we are conducting ourselves according to the pulse of each other without losing the pulse of ourselves? To the pulse of each other that wants something without orchestration and to do so without accidentally saying something we kind of mean but don't mean all the way and then it comes out anyway like a threat. Do we mean to threat? Is it dishonest to say that we never mean to threat? My treatment was supposed to make me more capable of assessing this, but have I gotten any closer? It's hard to get across how important it is for us now to orchestrate without making the whole point of orchestrating seem like it didn't matter at all. Because it won't matter if we are just clocking in this rest after all. So we can't pretend anymore and because of this it seems we keep on fighting.

You want to tune things out. You try. Maybe is it that I know I'm not supposed to react a certain way but I feel the bubbling inside of me and maybe I know it's wrong to let any sort of bubbling allow me to do something to someone but I also know it's something that someone else has once done to me and maybe I feel a certain resentment and I feel a separation, I feel how could could you why couldn't you... (/) Wasn't I someone who liked to go slowly too, aisle to aisle, wasn't I someone who tried to be aimless before? But if you even hint at it, if you even say aimless to the wrong person, it could and will be misconstrued like you are accusing. What for one person is a miracle for another person is the single worst thing possible. Is that what we've been working on?

There is a gift shop somewhere in relation to the main street but it is unclear whether this gift shop is to commemorate in the form of miniatures or to parallel in the from of true-to-life memorabilia. The gift shop is under threat even though the gift shop already exists. I have been putting off deciding whether or not I will contribute to the gift shop and by contribute I mean be the sole proprietor and by be the sole proprietor I mean do my little thing. Why do we want to be in a single place where everything we could need would be taken care of? Not that the gift shop would do this, in many ways the gift shop is everything we don't need plus a few things we might need, plus a few things we grow to start needing.

So someone got lost in there, someone got lost and someone else got caught waiting like someone else was clueless, not aimless, clueless, there is a difference, to have aims but not to have a single clue, and the other way around. I am very concerned right now for example about something I have always been concerned about except before when I was concerned I let it boil over immediately and I wouldn't let myself carry it with me, I would allow it to boil over and out of me. Now when I am concerned I wait, pace around,

I wait outside of the storefront or of whatever building, and I carry it for as long as I can. And until... And as I carry it, something happens... Maybe I find the clue back to my own aimlessness that got away... But what you carry never goes away...

Why do we look at something and confuse a mode of self-defense for something we can copy? We look at something and we look long enough to learn something about it but what we learn is not about what they see, it's about what we see of them, what we learn is what we might be able to copy of them, but what we learn to copy of them isn't a mode of self-defense, it becomes twisted into something we think we can wear, it becomes twisted into something we think we can wear and go anywhere, go anywhere like this... So it is no longer self-defense. It becomes preemptive, it becomes something that we use to threaten. I can't believe we look at something that is so hard to see and rather than think, what a miracle we can see it now, what a miracle we cannot see what they see, we think we have learned enough. Look... a rainbow...

When nothing happens, that's when everything happens. When too much is happening, that's when that nothing you could never take in your hands anyway, not when you most want to anyway, becomes something that's there, threatened, right in front of you. No, it's not that either. No... you still can't hold it but you can see it, it's right there... And that's when my heart goes bum bum bum, that's when I say, just to be upfront, it won't happen today, I'm washed over(,) sorry, today... That's when news comes through... Inflation(!)... That's when the neighbors are cussing and fighting and throwing their baby—they have a baby(?)—through the glass, strong head... That's when the probing leads to the bushes by the mulberry tree, by the mulberry tree near or around the mailbox... That's when they probe, probe(!)... That's when the rodents start making their little rodent cries and we hear them crying in the flooded basement and we start wondering whether and when they will ever checkin again on us... if they have been made aware, the ones who checkin on us... That's when I set out (   ) and (   ) but why... That's when you have to ask, are you home? are you home? or is the house just once again falling apart? That's when the lighting... That's when the hair... That's when the shedding of the hair... That's when the lightning... That's when kissing happens and good luck, good luck... That's when you stop looking right above you to see the fire coming down... That's when you stop wondering too.

Sometimes what you lose doesn't hurt, it doesn't hurt, it hurts you, you realize not until a long time after and even then when it's realized, you don't realize it, it's just realized... a long time after. (///////////////) One would hold onto things. In a way

I tried to. (   ) But couldn't. One would hold onto things longer than I ever could. What point would there be to compare this holding with anyone or thing else outside of us, beyond us, what point is there to compare, what would that do for what we could do? What could be changed if I could actually hold onto something longer than I did, than I ever have? What could have changed if one couldn't do that? One could do that so well...

ACKNOWLEDGMENTS

This book never would have come to be were it not for one fateful conversation with Hoa Nguyen.

I am also indebted to: Anselm Berrigan, Mónica de la Torre, Bill Dietz, Yasmine Eid-Sabbagh, Renee Gladman, Katherine Hubbard, Laura Huertas Millán, Anna Moschovakis, Ulrike Müller, Christopher Rey Perez, Beatriz Santiago Muñoz, Cedar Sigo, Kianja Strobert, Roberto Tejada, and Simone White — for the exchanges that followed.

Along the way, words of encouragement kept me warm from: Riel Bellow, Iara Carmen Hidalgo, Aristilde Kirby, Dani Lessnau, Funto Omojola, Sarah Passino, Andrea Sisson, Shaheen Qureshi, Katz Tepper, Nora Treatbaby, and Drew Zeiba.

I am also forever touched by conversations on writing and living shared with Raven Chacon, Rachel Simone

James, Ginger Ko, Okkyung Lee, Angie Sijun Lou, Jennifer Moon, Sondra Perry, and Halsey Rodman.

Thank you to Soham Patel & the editors of *Georgia Review* for sharing some of this book with your readers, and again to Anna Moschovakis in the capacity as my editor and to everyone at Ugly Duckling Presse who helped make this what it is.

The Naif
© 2024 Valerie Hsiung

ISBN 978-1-946604-25-5
Library of Congress Control Number 2023950182
First Printing, 2024

Published by Ugly Duckling Presse
Brooklyn, NY

This book is set in Input Sans

Design & typesetting by goodutopian
Cover designed & printed letterpress by IngeInge
Printed & bound at Sheridan (Saline, MI)

This project is supported, in part, by the New York State Council on the Arts with the support of the Office of the Governor and the New York State Legislature, by a Poetry Programs, Partnerships, and Innovation grant from the Poetry Foundation, and by an award from the National Endowment for the Arts.